Lake Erie and western railroad company. New York

Summer Excursion Routes through the most picturesque

Scenery in America

Seaside, Forest, Camp and watering Place

Lake Erie and western railroad company. New York

Summer Excursion Routes through the most picturesque Scenery in America
Seaside, Forest, Camp and watering Place

ISBN/EAN: 9783337144203

Printed in Europe, USA, Canada, Australia, Japan

Cover: Foto ©Andreas Hilbeck / pixelio.de

More available books at **www.hansebooks.com**

SUMMER EXCURSION ROUTES.

SEASIDE, FOREST, CAMP AND WATERING PLACE.

PHILADELPHIA
SUNSHINE PUBLISHING COMPANY,
306 and 308 Chestnut Street.
1881.

INDEX TO EXCURSIONS.

Alexandria Bay.. ... 30, 34, 36
Au Sable Chasm... 82
Albany.............. 82

Boston............. 76

Chautauqua Lake..... ....28, 29, 30
Clayton and Thousand Island Park (Alexandria
  Bay Excursions)........................34
Cleveland.................................16
Clifton Springs...........................28
Cooperstown...............................18
Crawford House (White Mountains Excursions) 52

Duluth....................................84

Erie Switchback....................14, 16, 78
Elmira....................................82

Fabyan House (White Mountains Excursions)... 52

Geneva (Seneca Lake)..................25, 82
Glen House (White Mountains Excursions).....52

Ha Ha Bay.................................84
Hammondsport (Niagara Falls Excursions Nos.
  16 and 17).............................12
Havana Glen...............................24
Hoosac Tunnel (Saratoga Excursions).......22

Ithaca................................24, 25

Jamestown (Chautauqua Lake Excursions)....29

Keuka Lake (Niagara Falls Excursions Nos.
  16 and 17).............................12

Lake Champlain and Lake George............82

Lake Side Resorts.........................96
Lake Couchiching..........................84
Lake Superior Tours.......................84
Lackawaxen................................78

Mayville (Chautauqua Lake Excursions).....29
Marquette.................................84
Mauch Chunk...............................82
Mauch Chunk Switchback....................82
Montreal................36, 40, 42, 46, 48, 72
Mt. Washington (White Mountains Excursions) 60
Mountain Resorts..........................90

Niagara Falls....................10, 11, 12

Oil Regions of Pennsylvania (Chautauqua Lake
  Excursions).............................30
Ottawa (Montreal Excursions Nos. 74 and 75) 42

Portland..................................76
Profile House (White Mountains Excursions) 60

Quebec.........................48, 49, 76, 84

Richfield Springs.........................18
Resorts for Sportsmen.....................91

Saratoga..............................22, 72
Sault Ste. Marie..........................84
Seneca Lake (Geneva and Watkins' Excursions) 82
Sharon Springs............................22
Switchback — Erie..................14, 16, 78

Taughannock Falls.........................28
Trenton Falls....................18, 22, 82

Watkins' Glen.....................22, 75, 78
White Mountains...........52, 54, 58, 60, 64, 66

Lake Minnewaska and Minnewaska Heights.

ASIDE from the wealth of the country presented to the seeker after summer pleasure in near by places, the Erie Railway is unsurpassed as a general route for the tourist. The number of its immediate attractions that are famous is very large, and in the convenient connections it makes with other routes for contiguous resorts the Erie is not approached by any other line. The whole route of the road is a continuous panorama of the grandest scenery, and the simple tour of the Erie alone is a source of constant pleasure to the traveler who truly loves the beautiful in nature. There are few stations on the line that have not some renowned attraction to the tourist.

Elsewhere in this book will be found more particular mention of attractive points within 180 miles of New York, or as far west as Hancock, on the Delaware Division.

From Hancock the road follows the Delaware to Deposit, with the same wild scenery abounding on both sides of the river. A short distance beyond Deposit it passes away from the Delaware Valley, and climbs the eastern side of the Randolph Hill which divide the Delaware from the Susquehanna. It is eight miles to the summit, where the road is nearly 1,400 feet above tide, and as the train thunders down the western slope, the tourist can scarcely bring himself to believe that a half hour ago he was skirting the romantic Delaware Highlands, and that now the picturesque portals of the Susquehanna Valley are opening before him, at a spot where nature has scattered her treasures with a prodigal hand. This is Starrucca, Susquehanna County, Pa. Before the train reaches the foot of the mountain, the great sweep of the road permits a general glimpse of Starrucca. The Viaduct—one of the grandest engineering feats in this country—its eighteen great arches supported by tall and graceful pillars; the Starrucca creek; the glorious curve of the Susquehanna, all fall beneath the delighted gaze. On the left hand, Elk Hill and Mount Ararat loom up in bold outline along the Starrucca. Gentle declivities rise beyond the Susquehanna, ridge after ridge. Starrucca Viaduct carries the Erie Railway over the valley of that name at a height of 110 feet. It is 1,200 feet long, and, with the charming setting of the landscape about it, formed the subject of one of the most famous of American paintings, "An American Autumn," by Cropsey. The most imposing view of the Viaduct is had from beneath, where the full immensity of its proportions are presented to the visitor with striking effect. The railroad running in under the Viaduct and up the Susquehanna Valley is the Nineveh Branch of the Albany and Susquehanna Railway.

Susquehanna Depot, a mile beyond the Viaduct, is the Western terminus of the Delaware Division, and the eastern extremity of the Susquehanna Division of the Erie. The Jefferson Branch runs from this place up the Starrucca Valley to Carbondale, in the northern anthracite coal fields of Pennsylvania, distant 38 miles. The railroad follows the Susquehanna Valley for 40 miles, crossing the river half a mile beyond Susquehanna Depot. Re-entering New York near Kirkwood, Broome County, it extends the remainder of the route, through the valleys and over the hill and streams of that State alone.

At Binghamton the Erie Railway connects with the Albany and Susquehanna Railway, for Saratoga Springs, Albany, Troy, Sharon Springs, Cooperstown, Howe's Cave, and Skeneatles Lake, and the cavernous wonders of Cobleskill and that part of Schoharie County; and with the Delaware, Lackawanna and Western for the Pennsylvania coal regions, Utica, Richfield's Springs, and Owego.

At Owego, Tioga County, the Erie Railway connects with a branch of the Delaware and Lackawanna Railway for Ithaca and *Cayuga Lake*. The region about Ithaca is famous for its cataracts, there being at least one hundred, ranging from 20 to 150 feet high, within an area of a few miles of the city, some of them being very near. This is one of the most attractive spots in southern New York. Owego was formerly the residence of N. P. Willis, and "Glen Mary," as his home was called by him, is still pointed out with no little local pride.

Near Waverly, Tioga County, the Susquehanna River sweeps away to the southward, and the Chemung Valley is entered. At Waverly connection is made with the Lehigh Valley Railroad for Philadelphia and the South. The Chemung River flows south from Waverly, and unites with the Susquehanna seven miles distant, in Bradford County, Pennsylvania. The place of junction was a favorite rendezvous of the Indians a hundred years ago. There the Tories and Indians arranged the details of the Wyoming massacre, and it was also the spot selected by General Washington as the meeting place of the armies of Generals Clinton and Sullivan, on their way to chastise the Indians after the Wyoming and Minisink massacres. The "castle" of the Indian Queen, Catharine Montour, was at Tioga Point. Near Waverly are the ruins or remains of what is believed to be an ancient military embankment. It is known to have been there nearly 200 years, and it was a ruin when first discovered. It is called the Spanish Hill, and

there are many theories as to its origin. Waverly is in both New York and Pennsylvania.

Elmira is the point from which Watkins and Havana Glens, Seneca Lake, and Crooked or Keuka Lake, in Yates and Schuyler Counties, New York, and the popular watering-place, Minequa Springs, in Bradford County, Pennsylvania, are reached by the Northern Central Railway. No excursion is complete unless it includes Watkins' Glen, with it unrivaled cataracts, its tremendous gorges, and its general wild surroundings, now so celebrated; and no one would think of leaving Watkins without making the round of the lakes mentioned. The best trout steams of the northern tier of Pennsylvania counties are also in close proximity to Elmira. The surroundings of the city are superb. It lies in the fairest part of Chemung Valley, with prominent hills extending around it on every side. Eldridge Park, the magnificent gift made by the late Dr. Edwin Eldridge to the city, is the finest public ground in the State, outside of New York and Brooklyn.

Corning, Steuben County, is the point from which the ROCHESTER DIVISION of the Erie Railway extends through the splendid section lying in the counties of Steuben, Livingston and Monroe. The semi-bituminous coal fields of Tioga County, Pennsylvania, are connected with the Erie at Corning. The valley of Chemung commences two miles west of Corning, the Conhocton and Tioga Rivers joining there and forming the Chemung. The Rochester Division follows the Conhocton Valley through Steuben to the border of Livingston County, and the Genesee Valley to Rochester through the latter county and Monroe.

At Bath, twenty miles from Corning, the Bath and Hammondsport Railway, a novel narrow guage road, runs to the western extremity of Keuka Lake, at Hammondsport, eight miles distant, in the centre of the great grape-growing region of Central New York. Blood's station thirty-nine miles from Corning is the connecting point for the beautiful *Canandaigua Lake* and its romantic surroundings. At Wayland, the summit of the ridge that is the dividing line between the water that flows into the Susquehanna basin and those finding the valley of the Genesee, is passed. The western border of the great wheat growing country of the Genesee is reached at

Livonia. This is the station from which *Hemlock, Conesus, Honeoye, Canadice* and other charming lakes of this region are reached. Conesus and Hemlock are within five miles of the station, and are two of the best fishing-grounds in the state. Conesus Lake is nine miles long, 300 feet deep, and of remarkable transparency. The muscalonge caught in these lakes are noted for their great size and fine flavor. The scenery around them is of the wildest kind.

Avon Springs, Livingston County, New York, on the Rochester Division, is a place famous for its sulphur Springs, which are unexcelled in valuable medicinal qualities by any waters in the country, rheumatics being especially benefited by them. Here is the heart of the *Genesee Valley*. On the banks of the Genessee, opposite Avon, is the site of the ancient Indian village, Canawagus. This was a favorite stopping-place of Red Jacket, who was a habitual partaker of the waters of the springs. From Avon connection may be made with the Buffalo Division at Attica, and the lower Genesee Valley at Mount Morris and Danville—sections of the greatest interest to tourist. On the branch extending to Attica, near the antique village of Caledonia, are the State Hatching Houses for the propagation of fish, for the purpose of stocking depleted waters in any part of the State. The spring that furnishes the water for this purpose is a great curiosity, covering as it does several acres with its cold and crystal water. The temperature of this water never changes. Caledonia is seven miles from Avon.

Rochester, the end of this Division, is a city of mills, of nurseries, and celebrated natural attractions. The falls of the Genesee thunder in the heart of the city. These great falls are among the wonders of the continent. At Rochester the bulk of the immense wheat yield of the Genesee Valley is manufactured. Lake Ontario is but four or five miles distant. Days may be spent in and about Rochester without exhausting the attractions of the locality.

Returning to Corning, on the main line, the *Canisteo Valley* is followed for forty miles, through a section of country of noted trout streams. At *Hornellsville* the Susquehanna Division of the Erie terminates, and the Western and Buffalo Division begins. The BUFFALO DIVISION runs to the northwest, through one of the finest sections of the State. At *Portage*, on this Division, the tourist will find himself in the midst of scenes whose grandeur deserves more than a passing notice. The broad vale of the Genesee river changes to a narrow and precipitous gorge, whose walls of solid rock tower in places four hundred feet above the stream, which roars and struggles in foaming fury to escape from its prison, and reach once more the fertile plains.

Here much of the savage grandeur of the scenes just mentioned is spread out before the tourist—the rush and roar of the water, the hoary heights, the out-spreading valley in the distance.

Six miles from *Gainesville* station, Wyoming County, on this Division is *Silver Lake*, a popular and charming summer resort.

At *Attica* the Avon Branch of the Rochester Division joins the Buffalo Division.

Buffalo, at the head of Niagara River, and on the eastern extremity of Lake Erie, is a point at and around which the visitor will find many new and surprising attractions.

From Buffalo the road passes on toward that Mecca of nine-tenths of the excursionists on this continent—*Niagara Falls*—twenty-five miles farther on. The visitor alights from the Erie Railway train in the very midst of the spray and thunder and terrific grandeur of this most stupendous fall of waters in the known world, "upon whose forehead God has set His rainbow, and mantled the clouds at its feet." Both writer and painter have bewailed the paucity of language and the inadequacy of art, when they have been called to treat of Niagara. The pen of Ruskin, or the pencil of a Turner, might so depict its glories as to awaken warm emotions in any breast; but they would, even in years of contemplation, evoke but a modicum of the overwhelming wonder that a moment face to face with the maniac waters will inspire. The description of Niagara and its surroundings is familiar to every school boy or girl. The ablest pens and pencils have set its features before the mind's eye; but it has been left for the Erie, by means of its remarkable thoroughfare, to bring the Falls themselves within easy reach of all who desire to witness their wonders. The tourist may now eat a five o'clock dinner in New York; take the Fast St. Louis Express on the Erie an hour later; enjoy a refreshing night's rest in a palace sleeping-coach; and eat his breakfast amid the roar of Niagara.

A LANDSCAPE.

I reach'd a height
Which lay from tinny fens to stately tree
Asleep in sunshine. From its crown I saw
The country fade into the distant sky,
With happy hamlets drown'd in apple bloom,
And ivy-muffled churches still with graves,
And restless fires subdued and tamed by day,
And scatter'd towns, whence came at intervals,
Upon the wind, a sweet clear sound of bells;
Through all, a river, like a stream of haze,
Drew its slow length until 'twas lost in woods.
Still as a lichen'd stone I lay and watch'd
The lights and shadows on the landscape's face,
The moving cloud that quench'd the shining fields,
The gliding sunbeam, the grey trailing shower,
And all the commerce of the earth and sky.

AN IRISH STORY.

A PROMINENT jeweler named West, had a handsome private residence in Harcourt Street, Dublin, and he was known habitually to place an unlimited confidence in the care and discretion of his wife, to leave large sums in her custody, and to approve of or acquiesce in the investments to which she might apply such moneys. Her management fully justified his confidence, and he made no secret of the course he had adopted or of the satisfactory results it produced. In 1876 he had arrived one morning in Skinner Row, when a livery servant of very stylish appearance, entered and enquired, "Had Captain Wilson been there?" Mr. West replied "he had not the pleasure of knowing Captain Wilson;" and then the servant stated, that "his master, Captain Marmaduke Wilson, intended to purchase some plate, and ordered him to go to Mr. West's and await his arrival there." He added, "He is a very fine looking man, but he has lost his right arm in the Crimea. I have to deliver a message in Dame Street. You will easily know him when he comes; and please to tell him that I shall be back in about ten minutes." The servant departed, and very soon after his master made his appearance. A complete *militaire*, he displayed moustaches, and a frogged frock coat; but the right sleeve was empty from the elbow, and the cuff was looped up to the breast. He inquired for the servant, and seemed a little dissatisfied at the fellow's absence. He then proceeded to inform Mr. West that he was about to fix his residence on a property which he held in the county of Monaghan, and that he wished to unite economy with respectability in his domestic arrangements. He had heard that Mr. West's stock of second-hand plate was very ample, and wished to purchase some on which the crestings could be obliterated and the Wilson crest substituted, producing at the same time a silver snuff-box, on which a crest was engraved, with the initials of Marmaduke Wilson beneath it. The servant had returned, and accompanied his master through the warerooms, conducted by the proprietor, who succeeded in displaying tea services, salvers, &c., which met with Captain Wilson's approval, provided the prices were lower. The demands were reduced considerably, as the customer urged that it was a dealing for "cash down." The charges amounted to one hundred and forty pounds, when the Captain said "he would not go any further for the present," and requested Mr. West to have the plate packed in a basket which the servant had brought, in order that Mrs. Wilson might see the articles before the crests were altered. The silver was directed to be treated as he desired, and he then turned to Mr. West and said, "You must be my amanuensis, and write the order to Mrs. Wilson for the cash. I shall send my man for the money, and when he brings it, you will leave him have the basket." Mr. West took the pen, and wrote, at the Captain's dictation—

"DEAR MARIA.

"I have bought some second-hand plate, of which, I think, you will approve. Send me, by bearer, £140."

He added—"Just put my initials, M. W. Is it not very curious, Mr. West, that our initials are the same?" He then took the pen in his left hand, and made a rough kind of small semi circle in the left-hand corner, which he designated his private mark. "Now," said he to the servant, "make all haste to your mistress, get the money, and fetch it here. I shall wait until you return, for you have not far to go." The servant departed, and the Captain remained for about twenty minutes, and seemed very impatient at the fellow's delay. He expressed an opinion that perhaps his wife had gone out, and said that he would take a car and see what caused the delay, adding, "When he brings you the cash you can let him have the hamper." The Captain then departed,

The servant did not come for the plate, and it remained packed and ready for delivery on the arrival of the purchase money. Late in the afternoon Mr. West went home, and having dined, was asked by his wife, "What second-hand plate was it that you bought to day?" "I bought none," he replied, "but I sold some, and it was to have been taken away at once, but I suppose it will be sent for to-morrow." "And why," enquired Mrs. West, "did you send to me for one hundred and forty pounds? Here is your note, which a servant in livery brought, and I gave him the money."

The swindle was complete. The basket was never called for, nor could the defrauded party ever obtain any trace of the Crimea Captain or of his livery servant. The reader need not suppose that the veteran delinquent was minus an arm. He was "made up" for the part which he was to play in the deliberate and deeply-planned villainy, and in all probability he had both his hands full of use, to take off his moustache and frogged coat in a very few minutes after leaving Mr. West's premises. The transaction excited much interest and some merriment. It afforded a subject for many jokes. He said that whether the captain reappeared or not, he could never be designated otherwise than as *off-handed* in his dealings with Mr. West.

MRS. BROWN.

It was up in old Kaintuck,
And his name was Billy Fry
And he fired a rock at Lucy
Brown and hit her in the eye.

And when Bijah brought him out the little nig. rolled up his eyes, drew down the corners of his mouth, and said:

"Say, boss, dat stone slipped. I was gwine to frow at a blue-jay on a telegraf-pole, but de stone flew off de handle an' hit Missus Brown. I tole her so all de time, but she got to ravin' aroun, an' gin me away to de poleece. She's mad at me 'bout our dorg an' her hens, an' dat's why she wanted me locked up."

"Now, h'ar dat young liar gon on!" exclaimed the indignant Mrs. Brown, who was present as a witness. "Why, boss, he frowed jiss as straight at me as he could, an' if I hadn't seen de rock comin' it would hev hit me on top de head. Ueah am de missive.

She exhibited a cobblestone weighing about six pounds, and asserted that it was the identical stone which hit her left eye. The rat of a prisoner looked from the stone to the Judge and said:

"Now, boss, I leaves it to you if I could frow dat rock across dis room? Why, if I'd hit her in de eye wid dat, she'd hev gone dead in a minit!"

"Boy, you go home, and don't you throw any more stones," replied the court as he closed the case.

"An' won't he be sent up?" asked the woman.

"No."

"All right!" she whispered as she followed the boy out. "If dat chile doan' git hisself spanked de worst way 'fore sundown to-night, den it's, kase he kin outrun de hull fam'ly!"

"SUPPOSE we pass a law," said a severe father to his daughters, "that no girl eighteen years old who can't cook a good meal, shall get married until she learns how to do it?" "Why, then we'll all get married at seventeen," responded the girls in sweet chorus.

"GOT all kinds of ties here?" said a would-be wit, entering a well-known furnishing store. "Yes sir," replied the shopman. "Well, I would like a pig sty," remarked the customer. "All right, sir; just bend down your hogshead, and we will take your measure," said the ready shopman.

A NOTED miser, who felt obliged to make a present to a lady, entered a crockery store for the purpose of making a purchase. Seeing a statuette broken into a dozen pieces, he asked the price. The salesman said it was worthless; but he could have it for the cost of packing in a box. The miser directed it to be sent, with his card, to the lady, congratulating himself that she would imagine that it was broken while on its way to her. He dropped in to see the effect. The tradesman had carefully wrapped each piece in a separate piece of paper. Tableau!

I WAS showing my watch to my nephew, who was about six years old. He pointed to the face of the dial, and said, "Why there is another little watch." I said, "That is called the second-hand." He tossed his head contemptuously and walked off, saying, "I wouldn't own a *second-hand* watch."

View of the Delaware at Hancock, Erie Railway.

I.
Excursions Starting from and Returning to New York.

NIAGARA FALLS.

EXCURSION No. 1.
New York to Niagara Falls, and return.

		MILES.
New York, Lake Erie and Western Railroad (via Avon Springs or Portage)	to Niagara Falls	443
New York, Lake Erie and Western Railroad (via Avon Springs or Portage)	to New York	443
Rate,	**$17.00**	

EXCURSION No. 2.
New York to Niagara Falls, and return.

		MILES.
New York, Lake Erie and Western Railroad (via Avon Springs or Portage)	to Niagara Falls	443
New York Central and Hudson River R. R.	to Albany	296
Day Line Hudson River Steamers	to New York	142
Rate,	**$17.00**	

EXCURSION No. 3.
New York to Niagara Falls, and return.

		MILES.
New York, Lake Erie and Western Railroad (via Avon Springs or Portage)	to Niagara Falls	443
New York Central and Hudson River R. R.	to New York	448
Rate,	**$17.75**	

EXCURSION No. 4.
New York to Niagara Falls and return.

		MILES.
New York, Lake Erie and Western Railroad (via Avon Springs or Portage)	to Niagara Falls	443
New York, Lake Erie and Western Railroad (via Avon Springs or Portage)	to Binghamton	228
Susquehanna Div., Del. & Hud. C. Co's Lines	to Albany	142
Day Line Hudson River Steamers	to New York	142
Rate,	**$17.00**	

EXCURSION No. 5.
New York to Niagara Falls and return.

		MILES.
Day Line Hudson River Steamers	to Albany	142
New York Central and Hudson River R. R.	to Niagara Falls	296
New York, Lake Erie and Western Railroad (via Avon Springs or Portage)	to New York	443
Rate,	**$17.00**	

EXCURSION No. 6.
New York to Niagara Falls and return.

		MILES.
New York, Lake Erie and Western Railroad	to Elmira	274
Northern Central Railway (via Watkins' Glen)	to Canandaigua	69
New York Central and Hudson River Railroad	to Niagara Falls	106
New York, Lake Erie and Western Railroad (via Avon Springs or Portage)	to New York	443
Rate,	**$17.50**	

EXCURSION No. 7.
New York to Niagara Falls and return.

		MILES.
New York, Lake Erie and Western Railroad (via Avon Springs or Portage)	to Niagara Falls	443
New York Central and Hudson River R. R. (via Clifton Springs)	to Geneva	150
Seneca Lake Steamer	to Watkins	40
Northern Central Railway	to Elmira	92
New York, Lake Erie and Western Railroad	to New York	274
Rate,	**$17.75**	

Niagara Falls.

EXCURSION No. 8.
New York to Niagara Falls and return.

	MILES.
New York, Lake Erie and Western Railroad *via* Avon Springs or Portage	to Niagara Falls...... 443
New York Central and Hudson River R. R.	to Albany............ 296
Saratoga Div., Del. & Hud. C. Co's Lines.	to Saratoga........... 38
Saratoga Div., Del. & Hud. C. Co's Lines.	to Albany............. 38
Day Line Hudson River Steamers.	to New York.......... 142

Rate, - $19.10

EXCURSION No. 9.
New York to Niagara Falls and return.

	MILES.
Day Line Hudson River Steamers.	to Albany............ 142
Saratoga Div., Del. & Hud. C. Co's Lines.	to Saratoga........... 38
Saratoga Div., Del. & Hud. C. Co's Lines.	to Schenectady....... 21
New York Central and Hudson River R. R.	to Niagara Falls..... 289
New York, Lake Erie and Western Railroad (*via* Avon Springs or Portage	to New York.......... 443

Rate, - - - - $18.25

EXCURSION No. 10.
New York to Niagara Falls and return.

	MILES.
New York, Lake Erie and Western Railroad *via* Avon Springs or Portage	to Niagara Falls...... 442
New York Central and Hudson River R. R.	to Utica............. 211
Delaware, Lackawanna and Western R. R.	to Richfield Springs 35
Stage and Otsego Lake Steamer.	to Cooperstown...... 16
Cooperstown and Susquehanna Valley R. R.	to Junction.......... 16
Susquehanna Div., D. & H. C. Co's Lines.	to Albany............ 75
Day Line Hudson River Steamers.	to New York......... 142

Rate, $18.65

EXCURSION No. 11.
New York to Niagara Falls and return.

	MILES.
New York, Lake Erie and Western Railroad [*via* Avon Springs or Portage	to Niagara Falls..... 443
New York, Lake Erie and Western Railroad [*via* Avon Springs or Portage	to Binghamton...... 228
Susquehanna Div., D. & H. C. Co's Lines.	to Junction.......... 67
Cooperstown and Susquehanna Valley R. R.	to Cooperstown..... 16
Cooperstown and Susquehanna Valley R. R.	to Junction.......... 16
Susquehanna Div., D. & H. C. Co's Lines.	to Albany............ 75
Day Line Hudson River Steamers.	to New York......... 142

Rate, - - $18.20

EXCURSION No. 12.
New York to Niagara Falls and return.

	MILES.
New York, Lake Erie and Western Railroad [*via* Avon Springs or Portage]	to Niagara Falls .. 443
New York, Lake Erie and Western Railroad (*via* Avon Springs or Portage)	to Binghamton...... 228
Susquehanna Div., D. & H. C. Co's Lines.	to Sharon Springs 111
Susquehanna Div., D. & H. C. Co's Lines.	to Albany........... 59
Day Line Hudson River Steamers.	to New York........ 142

Rate, - - - $17.60

EXCURSION No. 13.
New York to Niagara Falls and return.

	MILES.
Day Line Hudson River Steamers.	to Albany............ 142
Susquehanna Div., Del. & Hud. C. Co's Lines.	to Sharon Springs .. 59
Susquehanna Div., Del. & Hud. C. Co's Lines.	to Cherry Valley.. 9
Stage and Otsego Lake Steamers.	to Cooperstown..... 16
Otsego Lake Steamer and Stage.	to Richfield Springs. 16
Delaware, Lackawanna and Western R. R.	to Utica............. 35
New York Central and Hudson River R. R.	to Niagara Falls... 211
New York, Lake Erie and Western Railroad *via* Avon Springs or Portage	to New York........ 443

Rate, - - - - $19.00

Niagara Falls.

EXCURSION No. 14.
New York to Niagara Falls and return.

	MILES.
New York, Lake Erie, and Western Railroad (via Avon Springs or Portage)..................to Niagara Falls	443
New York Central and Hudson River R. R. (via Clifton Springs)..................to Cayuga	143
Cayuga Lake Steamers..................to Ithaca	38
Delaware, Lackawanna and Western R. R...................to Owego	33
New York, Lake Erie and Western Railroad..................to New York	237

Rate, - - - - $17.00

EXCURSION No. 15.
New York to Niagara Falls and return.

	MILES.
Day Line Hudson River Steamers..................to Albany	142
Susquehanna Div., Del. & Hud. C. Co's. Lines..................to Binghamton	142
New York, Lake Erie and Western Railroad (via Avon Springs or Portage)..................to Niagara Falls	228
New York, Lake Erie and Western Railroad, (via Avon Springs or Portage)..................to New York	443

Rate, - - - - $17.00

EXCURSION No. 16.
New York to Niagara Falls and return.

	MILES.
New York, Lake Erie and Western Railroad [via Avon Springs or Portage]..................to Niagara Falls	443
New York, Lake Erie and Western Railroad [via Avon Springs]..................to Bath	141
Bath and Hammondsport R. R...................to Hammondsport	9
Lake Keuka Steamer..................to Penn Yan	22
Northern Central Railway [via Watkins' Glen]..................to Elmira	45
New York, Lake Erie and Western Railroad..................to New York	274

Rate - - - 17.50

EXCURSION No. 17.
New York to Niagara Falls and return.

	MILES.
New York, Lake Erie and Western Railroad..................to Bath	311
Bath and Hammondsport R. R...................to Hammondsport	9
Lake Keuka Steamer..................to Penn Yan	22
Northern Central Railway..................to Canandaigua	24
New York Central and Hudson River R. R...................to Niagara Falls	106
New York, Lake Erie and Western Railroad [via Avon Springs or Portage]..................to New York	443

Rate, - - - - $18.00

EXCURSION No. 18.
New York to Niagara Falls and return.

	MILES.
New York, Lake Erie and Western Railroad [via Avon Springs or Portage]..................to Niagara Falls	443
New York, Lake Erie and Western Railroad [via Avon Springs or Portage]..................to Waverly	187
Lehigh Valley R. R...................to Mauch Chunk	160
Central R. R. of New Jersey..................to New York	121

Rate, - - - - $17.00

EXCURSION No. 19.
New York to Niagara Falls and return.

	MILES.
New York, Lake Erie and Western Railroad (via Avon Springs or Portage)..................to Niagara Falls	443
New York, Lake Erie and Western Railroad [via Avon Springs or Portage]..................to Binghamton	228
Delaware, Lackawanna and Western R. R. [via Water Gap]..................to New York	210

Rate - - - - $17.00

EXCURSION No. 20.
New York to Niagara Falls and return.

	MILES.
New York, Lake Erie and Western Railroad..................to Elmira	274
Northern Central Railway..................to Watkins'	22
Seneca Lake Steamer..................to Geneva	40
New York Central and Hudson River R. R. [via Clifton Springs]..................to Niagara Falls	129
New York, Lake Erie and Western Railroad [via Avon Springs or Portage]..................to New York	443

Rate, - - - - $17.75

THE ALARM.

His eye was stern and wild; his cheek
　Was pale and cold as clay;
Upon his tighten'd lip a smile
　Of fearful meaning lay.

I saw him bare his throat, and seize
　The blue, cold, gleaming steel,
And grimly try the temper'd edge
　He was so soon to feel.

Black icy horrors struck me dumb,
　And froze my senses o'er;
I closed my eyes in utter fear,
　And strove to think no more.

He raised on high the glittering blade;
　Then first I found a tongue:
"Hold, madman! stay the frantic deed!"
　I cried, and forth I sprung.

He heard me, but he heeded not;
　One glance around he gave;
And ere I could arrest his hand,
　He had—begun to shave!

FABLES FOR FOOLS.

A DOG being very much annoyed by bees, ran quite accidentally into an empty barrel, lying on the ground, and looking out at the bung-hole, addressed his tormentors thus:

"Had you been temperate, stinging me only one at a time, you might have got a good deal of fun out of me. As it is you have driven me into a secure retreat; for I can snap you up as fast as you come in through the bung-hole. Learn from this the folly of intemperate zeal."

When he had concluded he awaited a reply. There wasn't any reply; for the bees had never gone near the bung-hole; they went in the same way as he did, and made it very warm for him.

The lesson of this fable is that one cannot stick to his pure reason while quarrelling with bees.

SOME doves went to a hawk, and asked him to protect them from a kite.

"That I will," was the cheerful reply; "and when I am admitted into the dovecote I shall kill more of you in a day than the kite did in a century. But, of course, you know this; you expect to be treated in the regular way."

So he entered the dovecote, and began preparations for a general slaughter. But the doves all set upon him and made exceedingly short work of him. With his last breath he asked them why, being so formidable, they had not killed the kite. They replied that they had never seen any kite.

PEOPLE who wear tight hats will do well to lay this fable well to heart, and ponder upon the deep significence of its moral—

IN passing over a river, upon a high bridge, a cow discovered a broad, loose plank in the flooring, sustained in place by a beam beneath the centre.

"Now," said she, "I will stand at this end of the trap, and when yonder sheep steps upon the opposite extreme there will be an upward tendency in wool."

So, when the meditative mutton advanced, unwarily, upon the treacherous device, the cow sprang bodily upon the other end, and there was a fall in beef.

"AWFUL dark—isn't it?" said an owl, one night, looking in upon the roosting hens in a poultry house; "don't see how I am to find my way back to my hollow tree."

"There is no necessity," replied the cock; "you can roost there, alongside the door, and go home in the morning."

"Thanks!" said the owl, chuckling at the fool's simplicity; and, having plenty of time to indulge his facetious humor, he gravely installed himself upon the perch indicated, and shutting his eyes, counterfeited a profound slumber. He was aroused soon after by a sharp constriction of the throat.

"I omitted to tell you," said the cock, "that the seat you happen, by the merest chance, to occupy is a contested one, and has been fruitful of hens to this vexatious weasel. I don't know how often I have been partially widowed by the sneaking villian.

For obvious reasons there was no audible reply.

This narrative is intended to teach the folly the worse than sin—of trumping your partner's ace.

A FOX and a duck having quarrelled about the ownership of a frog, agreed to refer the dispute to a lion. After hearing a great deal of argument, the lion opened his mouth to speak.

"I am very well aware," interrupted the duck, "what your decision is. It is that by our own showing the frog belongs to neither of us, and you will eat him yourself. But, please remember that lions do not like frogs."

"To me," exclaimed the fox, "it is perfectly clear that you will give the frog to the duck, the duck to me, and take me yourself. Allow me to state certain objections to—"

"I was about to remark," said the lion, "that while you were disputing, the cause of contention had hopped away. Perhaps you can procure another frog."

THE ERIE SWITCHBACK.

NEW EXCURSION ROUTE.

The Moosic range of mountains is one of the loftiest spurs of the Alleghenies. Some of the peaks are 2,500 feet in height. The range is wild and rugged, and nowhere else in the State of Pennsylvania is the scenery grander or more diversified. Scaling its summits, spanning its chasms, and threading its dense forests, are two of the most novel railroads in the world. These are the Delaware and Hudson Canal Company's Gravity Road and the Gravity Road of the Pennsylvania Coal Company. These roads are operated by an ingenious system of inclined planes, up and down the mountain, there being no locomotive smoke nor cinders to annoy the tourists. The delightful character of a ride over these gravity roads cannot be conveyed by words. There is nothing like it in this country. The Pennsylvania Coal Company's road climbs from Dunmore, Pa., to a height of 2,100 feet in a distance of five miles. The road extends to Hawley, a distance of 33 miles, and then by another route back to Dunmore, one mile from Scranton. The Delaware and Hudson's gravity road extends from Honesdale to Carbondale, seventeen miles, and back by another route. The highest point on this road is 2,000 feet, and from the car windows the Catskill mountains may be seen, sixty miles away. Lakes, waterfalls, glens, and valleys make these two excursions by gravity unrivalled. The Erie Railway Company has made every arrangement to introduce these roads to the public this season. The accompanying schedule will give all information in regard to routes and rates of fare, while the map published in connection herewith will show at a glance the novelty of the excursion. Trains on these gravity roads connect with Erie Express trains to and from New York. Holders of other excursions, passing Lackawaxen at any portion of the route, can take in the ERIE SWITCHBACK at a trifling additional expense, by means of the Side Trip Extension Excursions T, W, Y, and Z.

ERIE SWITCHBACK.

EXCURSION No. 56.

New York to Carbondale and return, (Del. and Hud. C. Co's Gravity R. R.)

		MILES.
New York, Lake Erie and Western Railroad	to Honesdale	136
Omnibus	{ to Del. & Hud. C.) (Co's Depot........)	1
Del. and Hud. Canal Co's Gravity R. R.	to Carbondale	16
Del. and Hud. Canal Co's Gravity R. R.	to Honesdale	18
Stage	{ to Depot N. Y., L.) (E. & W. R. R.....)	1
New York, Lake Erie and Western Railroad	to New York	136
Rate,	$8.00	

EXCURSION No. 57.

New York to Dunmore (Scranton) and return, (Penna. Coal Co's Gravity R. R.)

		MILES.
New York, Lake Erie and Western Railroad	to Hawley	127
Penna. Coal Co's Gravity Railroad	to Dunmore	33
Penna. Coal Co's Gravity Railroad	to Hawley	33
New York, Lake Erie and Western Railroad	to New York	127
Rate,	$7.45	

EXCURSION No. 58.

New York to Scranton and return (Del. and Hud. C. Co's Gravity R. R. and Penna. Co's Gravity R. R.)

		MILES.
New York, Lake Erie and Western Railroad	to Honesdale	136
Omnibus	{ to Del. & Hud. C.) (Co's Depot........)	1
Del. and Hud. Canal Co's Gravity R. R.	to Carbondale	16
Omnibus	{ to Del. & Hud. C.) (Co's Depot........)	1
Penna. Division D. and H. C. Co's Lines.	to Scranton	16
People's Passenger Railway	to Dunmore	1½
Penna. Coal Co's Gravity R. R.	to Hawley	33
New York, Lake Erie and Western Railroad	to New York	127
Rate,	$8.25	

MODEL PUBLIC SERVANTS.
ERIE CONDUCTORS.

THE man who said he had heard of civil engineers, but never of civil conductors, was never a patron of the great Erie Railway. It is a rule on all railroads, we believe, that train employés shall maintain a respectful and courteous bearing toward passengers at all times, but men are not made gentlemen by rule. If a conductor is a boor, if he is surly and snappish by nature, no company rules can transform him into a courteous gentleman. He may not violate the letter of the rules made to govern him, and yet his bearing toward the people in his charge may be such as to repel and make them uncomfortable. We do not *know* it to be the case, but it seems to us that whoever has the filling of the responsible position of conductor with the men who occupy it on the Erie Railway, must realize this fact in making his appointments, for, ride on what train he may on this road—on the great divisions of the main line or the smallest and most unimportant branches—the traveler will meet with the same patient, kindly, attentive conductors in charge.

It is the mission of the Erie conductor to put every one in his charge at his or her ease until the journey is ended. He has not only his professional reputation to maintain, but his reputation as a gentleman, and he does not do it under the pressure of rules but from intuition. Politeness, patience, impartiality and care, are his cardinal virtues, and it gives us pleasure to commend him, individually and collectively, to the traveling public, and especially to the timid and nervous, the inexperienced, and the unprotected. In paying this deserved tribute to the conductors of the Erie, we would by no means be understood as disparaging many of the same class of officials on other roads, but we speak of the Erie from better opportunities for observation,

Erie Swithback—Cleveland.

EXCURSION No. 59.

New York to Scranton and return (Penna. Coal Co's Gravity R. R. and Del. and Hud. C. Co's Gravity R. R.)

	MILES.
New York, Lake Erie and Western Railroad...	...to Hawley................ 127
Penna. Coal Co's Gravity R. R......................	....to Dunmore............ 33
People's Passenger Railway..........................	...to Scranton........... 1½
Penna. Division, Del. and Hud. C. Co's Lines..	......to Carbondale........ 16
Omnibus	{ to Depot D. & H. C. } 1 { Co's Gravity R. R. }
Del. and Hud. Canal Co's Gravity R. R.	......to Honesdale........... 18
Omnibus	{ to Depot N. Y., L. } 1 { E. & W. R. R. }
New York, Lake Erie and Western Railroad....	............to New York.......... 136

Rate, - - - - $8.25

*Although Excursion No. 59 is the reverse of Excursion No. 58, it covers different ground, as Excursion No. 58 traverses only *one-half* of the round trip loop of each Gravity Road, while Excursion No. 59 traverses the *remaining half*.

CLEVELAND.

EXCURSION No. 63.
New York to Cleveland and return.

	MILES.
New York, Lake Erie and Western Railroad (via Avon Springs or Portage).....	.....to Niagara Falls..... 443
New York, Lake Erie and Western Railroad.....	....to Buffalo........... 23
Lake Shore and Michigan Southern Railway....	....to Cleveland.......... 183
Lake Shore and Michigan Southern Railway....	....to Buffalo............ 183
New York, Lake Erie and Western Railroad (via Avon Springs or Portage).....	....to New York........... 423

Rate, - - - - $27.00

EXCURSION No. 64.
New York to Cleveland and return.

	MILES.
New York, Lake Erie and Western Railroad via Avon Springs or Portage.....	....to Niagara Falls..... 443
New York, Lake Erie and Western Railroad.....	....to Buffalo........... 23
Lake Shore and Michigan Southern Railway.	....to Cleveland.......... 183
Atlantic and Great Western Railway.............	....to Salamanca......... 214
New York, Lake Erie and Western Railroad....	....to New York........... 414

Rate, - - - - $27.00

EXCURSION No. 65.
New York to Cleveland and return.

	MILES.
New York, Lake Erie and Western Railroad (via Avon Springs or Portage).........	....to Niagara Falls.... 443
New York, Lake Erie and Western Railroad.....	....to Buffalo.......... 23
Lake Shore and Michigan Southern Railway	....to Cleveland....... 183
Cleveland and Pittsburg R. R................	....to Pittsburg........ 150
Pennsylvania Railroad............................	....to New York......... 444

Rate, - - - $27.00

EXCURSION No. 66.
New York to Cleveland and return.

	MILES.
New York, Lake Erie and Western Railroad.......	....to Salamanca...... 414
Atlantic and Great Western Railway.............	....to Jamestown....... 34
Steamer on Chatauqua Lake.....................	....to Mayville......... 22
Steamer on Chatauqua Lake.....................	....to Jamestown....... 22
Atlantic and Great Western Railway............	....to Cleveland........ 180
Lake Shore and Michigan Southern Railway...	....to Buffalo.......... 183
New York, Lake Erie and Western Railroad.....	....to Niagara Falls.... 23
New York, Lake Erie and Western Railroad (via Avon Springs or Portage).	....to New York......... 443

Rate, - - - $27.75

THE WOODS.

There is a pleasure in the pathless woods,
There is a rapture on the lonely shore,
There is society where none intrudes,
By the deep sea, and music in its roar
I love not man the less, but nature more,
From these our interviews, in which I steal
From all I may be, or have been before,
To mingle with the universe, and feel
What I can ne'er express, yet cannot all conceal.

MUSICAL ACCENT.

AT a trial in the Court of King's bench between certain publishing tweedledums and tweedledees, as to an alleged piracy of an arrangement of "The Old English Gentlemen," T Cooke was subpœnaed as a witness. On cross examination by Sir James Scarlett, that learned counsel rather flippantly said, "Now, sir, you say the two melodies are the same but different. What do you mean, sir?" Tom promptly an-

A Shady Nook on the Erie.

swered, I said that the notes in the two copies were alike, but with a different accent." Sir James: "What is a musical accent?" Cooke: "My terms are a guinea a lesson, sir." A loud laugh. Sir James rather ruffled "Don't mind your terms here. I asked you what is a musical accent? Can you see it?" Cooke: "A musician can." Great laughter. Sir James very angrily : " Now, pray, sir, don't beat about the bush, but tell his lordship and the jury, who are supposed to know nothing about it, the meaning of what you call accent?" Cooke: "Accent in music is stress laid upon a particular note, as you would lay stress upon any given word, for the purpose of being better understood. If I were to say you are an *ass*, it rests on *ass*; but if I were to say *you* are an ass, it rests on *you*, Sir James." Reiterated shouts of laughter by the whole court, in which the bench joined, followed this repartee. Silence being obtained, Lord Denman, the judge, with much seeming gravity, accosted the chopfallen counsel, "Are you satisfied, Sir James?" Sir James, deep red as he naturally was, had become Scarlett in more than name; and, in a great huff, said, "The witness may go down."

A LITTLE girl hearing that her mother was going into half mourning, wished to know if any of her relatives were *half dead*.

Cooperstown—Richfield Springs—Trenton Falls.

COOPERSTOWN.

EXCURSION No. 21.
New York to Cooperstown and return.

		MILES.
New York, Lake Erie and Western Railroad	to Binghamton	215
Susquehanna Div., Del. & Hud. C. Co's Line	to Junction	67
Cooperstown and Susquehanna Valley Railroad	to Cooperstown	16
Cooperstown and Susquehanna Valley R. R.	to Junction	16
Susquehanna Div., Del. & Hud. C. Co's Lines	to Albany	75
Day Line Hudson River Steamers	to New York	142

Rate, - - - - $10.25

EXCURSION No. 22.
New York to Cooperstown and return.

		MILES.
Day Line Hudson River Steamers	to Albany	142
Susquehanna Div., Del. & H. C. Co's Lines	to Junction	75
Cooperstown and Susquehanna Valley R. R.	to Cooperstown	16
Cooperstown and Susquehanna Valley R. R.	to Junction	16
Susquehanna Div., Del. & Hud. C. Co's Lines	to Binghamton	67
New York, Lake Erie and Western Railroad	to New York	215

Rate, - - - - $10.25

RICHFIELD SPRINGS.

EXCURSION No. 23.
New York to Richfield Springs and return.

		MILES.
New York, Lake Erie and Western Railroad	to Binghamton	215
Delaware, Lackawanna and Western Railroad	to Richfield Springs	103
Stage and Otsego Lake	to Cooperstown	16
Cooperstown and Susquehanna Valley Railroad	to Junction	16
Susquehanna Div., Del. & Hud. C. Co's Lines	to Albany	75
Day Line Hudson River Steamers	to New York	142

Rate, - - - - $11.50

EXCURSION No. 24.
New York to Richfield Springs and return.

		MILES.
Day Line Hudson River Steamers	to Albany	142
New York Central and Hudson River Railroad	to Utica	95
Delaware, Lackawanna and Western Railroad	to Richfield Springs	35
Stage and Otsego Lake Steamers	to Cooperstown	16
Cooperstown and Susquehanna Valley Railroad	to Junction	16
Susquehanna Div., Del. & Hud. C. Co's Lines	to Binghamton	67
New York, Lake Erie and Western Railroad	to New York	215

Rate, - - - - $11.90

TRENTON FALLS.

EXCURSION No. 25.
New York to Trenton Falls and return.

		MILES.
New York, Lake Erie and Western Railroad	to Binghamton	215
Delaware, Lackawanna and Western Railroad	to Utica	95
Utica and Black River R. R.	to Trenton Falls	18
Utica and Black River R. R.	to Utica	18
Delaware, Lackawanna and Western Railroad	to Richfield Springs	35
Stage and Otsego Lake Steamer	to Cooperstown	16
Cooperstown and Susquehanna Valley Railroad	to Junction	16
Susquehanna Div., Del. & Hud. C. Co's Lines	to Albany	75
Day Line Hudson River Steamers	to New York	142

Rate, - - - - $13.25

A DINNER AND A KISS.

"I have brought your dinner, father,"
　The blacksmith's daughter said,
As she took from her arm the kettle
　And lifted its shining lid.
"There is not any pie or pudding,
　So I will give you this,"
And upon his toil-worn forehead
　She left the childish kiss.

The blacksmith took off his apron
　And dined in happy mood,
Wondering much at the savor
　Hid in his humble food;
While all about him were visions,
　Full of prophetic bliss;
But he never thought of magic
　In his little daughter's kiss.

While she, with her kettle swinging,
　Merrily trudged away,
Stopping at sight of a squirrel
　Catching some wild bird's lay.
And I thought how many a shadow
　Of life and fate we would miss,
If always our frugal dinners
　Were seasoned with a kiss.

CAMP-MEETING INCIDENT.

OUR readers may remember the story of the "soaping" of the signal horn. The story runs that when a certain revivalist celebrity took up the horn, to summon the worshippers to service, after dinner, one day, he blew a strong blast of soft soap all over the astonished brethren. It is also said by the chronicler of this "item" that the brother was so wroth at this joke that he cried out aloud, "Brethren, I have passed through many trials and tribulations, but nothing like this. I have served the ministry for thirty years, and in that time have never uttered a profane word, but I'll be cussed if I can't whip the man that soaped that horn."

Well, this is a story; but we have from a reliable authority, something a little stronger in the sequel to the same incident. This is given to us as follows:

Some two days after the horn-soaping, a tall, swarthy, villainous-looking desperado strolled on the grounds, and leaned against a tree, listening to the eloquent exhortation to repent which was being made by the preacher. After a while he became interested, finally affected, and then took a position on the anxious seat, commenced groaning in "the very bitterness" of his sorrow. The clergyman walked down and endeavored to console him. No consolation—he was too great a sinner, he said. Oh, no—there was pardon for the vilest. No, he was too wicked—there was no mercy for him.

"Why, what crime have you committed!" said the preacher; "have you stolen?"

"Oh, worse than that!"

"What! have you committed perjury?"

"Worse than that—oh, worse than that!"

"Murder, is it?" gasped the horrified preacher.

"Worse than that!" groaned the smitten sinner.

The excited preacher commenced "peeling off" his outer garments.

"Here, Brother Cole!" shouted he, "hold my coat—I've found the fellow that soaped that horn!"

"WHAT is wisdom?" asked a teacher of a class of small girls. A bright-eyed little creature arose and answered: "Information of the brain."

"JIM, kin you tell me de difference between a rotten head of cabbage and a watermelon?"

"No, sah."

"Well, for the land sakes, you'd be a nice nigger to send out to buy a watermelon! E'yah! e'yah!"

A GENTLEMAN without tact, on meeting some ladies whom he had known as girls in his boyhood, cordially remarked, "Bless me! How time flies! Let me see. It is thirty-two years come next April since we used to go to school together in the old red schoolhouse. I was a little chap then, you remember, and you were fine young women." The man could never understand why his cordial greeting was received so coldly.

"MIKE," said a priest to his servant, "if the protestant minister calls to-day, remember I do not wish to see him; don't say I am not at home, for that would be telling a lie, but give him an evasive answer." "Och, I will," said Mike. "Well, Mike," said the priest in the evening, "did the minister call?" "Faix, he did, your riverence." "What answer did you give him?" "I gave him an evasive answer, as your riverence towld me." "But what did you say to him?" "Why, your riverence, he axed me was yez at home, and I towld him, was his grandmother a donkey."

SUNSHINE PUBLISHING COMPANY. 306 & 308 CHESTNUT ST., PHILADELPHIA.

ESTABLISHED OVER TWENTY-EIGHT YEARS.

A. T. ZEISING & CO.

STEAM-POWER

BOOK AND JOB PRINTERS.

A. T. ZEISING & CO.,
PUBLISHERS.

Rev. J. HENRY SMYTHE, A. M.
EDITOR.

DELAWARE RIVER NEAR PORT JERVIS

On the Delaware River near Port Jervis, N. Y.

EXCURSION No. 26.
New York to Trenton Falls and return.

		MILES.
Day Line Hudson River Steamers	to Albany	142
New York Central and Hudson River R. R.	to Utica	95
Utica and Black River R. R.	to Trenton Falls	18
Utica and Black River R. R.	to Utica	18
Delaware, Lackawanna and Western R. R.	to Binghamton	95
New York, Lake Erie and Western Railroad	to New York	215

Rate, - - - - $11.25

SARATOGA.
EXCURSION No. 67.
New York to Saratoga and return.

		MILES.
New York, Lake Erie and Western Railroad	to Binghamton	215
Susquehanna Div., Del. and Hud. C. Co's Lines	to Albany	142
Saratoga Div., Del. and Hud. C. Co's Lines	to Saratoga	38
Saratoga Div., Del. and Hud. C. Co's Lines	to Mechanicville	32
Boston, Hoosac Tunnel and Western Railway	to North Adams	48
Fitchburgh R. R. (Hoosac Tunnel)	to Boston	143
Old Colony R. R.	to Newport	68
Fall River Line Steamers	to New York	162

Rate, - - - - $16.00

EXCURSION No. 68.
New York to Saratoga and return.

		MILES
Fall River Line Steamers	to Newport	162
Old Colony R. R.	to Boston	68
Fitchburgh R. R. (Hoosac Tunnel)	to North Adams	143
Boston, Hoosac Tunnel and Western Railway	to Mechanicville	48
Saratoga Div., Del. and Hud. C. Co's Lines	to Saratoga	32
Saratoga Div., Del. and Hud. C. Co's Lines	to Albany	38
New York, Lake Erie and Western Railroad	to Binghamton	142
Susquehanna Div., Del. & Hud. C. Co's Lines	to New York	215

Rate, - - - - $16.00

SHARON SPRINGS.
EXCURSION No. 27.
New York to Sharon Springs and return.

		MILES.
New York, Lake Erie and Western Railroad	to Binghamton	215
Susquehanna Div., Del. & Hud. C. Co's Lines	to Sharon Springs	111
Susquehanna Div., Del. & Hud. C. Co's Lines	to Albany	59
Day Line Hudson River Steamers	to New York	142

Rate, - - - - $9.65

EXCURSION No. 28.
New York to Sharon Springs and return.

		MILES.
Day Line Hudson River Steamers	to Albany	142
Susquehanna Div., Del. & Hud. C. Co's Lines	to Sharon Springs	59
Susquehanna Div., Del. & Hud. C. Co's Lines	to Binghamton	111
New York, Lake Erie and Western Railroad	to New York	215

Rate, - - - - $9.65

WATKINS' GLEN.
EXCURSION No. 29.
New York to Watkins' Glen and return.

		MILES.
New York, Lake Erie and Western Railroad	to Elmira	274
Northern Central Railway	to Watkins'	22
Northern Central Railway	to Elmira	22
New York, Lake Erie and Western Railroad	to New York	274

Rate, - - - - $11.75

VALLEY FORGE.

NO spot possesses a deeper interest for Americans than the long rolling highlands on the banks of the Schuylkill, so memorable in history as Valley Forge. Here was the army disposed, and if it had been properly provided with an efficient commissary department, the winter might have been passed in comparative comfort. But even had the rude log huts of the soldiers been transformed into palaces, the gnawing of hunger alone would have made them still wretched. Nothing is so fatal as the absence of good, nutritious food. We who are blessed by a kind Providence with all life's comforts, and who sit down every day to our well-ordered table, can have but a faint idea of the sufferings of our fellow-beings who are starving in some of the low dens of the city; and we can realize but feebly what the poor soldiers of Valley Forge endured. It was the darkest hour in all our revolutionary history.

Washington's room is preserved in precisely the same condition in which he kept it. In one of the deep window-seats is discovered a secret repository, which he used for his private papers. Several old cannon-balls were rolled out on the floor by the young lady who showed us the room, with the explanation that they were samples of many more which had been ploughed up in the fields.

From Washington's headquarters the ground gradually rises toward the south, and by gentle swells spreads out for over a mile, forming the camping-grounds where the log-barracks were erected. Surrounding these rolling meadows on the northwest are high bluffs, upon which was posted the main portion of the army.

Washington chose this position for the cantoning of his troops, not only because it was near enough to Philadelphia to keep a vigilant watch over that city, but also on account of its natural advantages, as it was well adapted for a strongly entrenched encampment, and had a good supply of fresh water always on hand.

It is situated at the entrance to the valley, in Chester county, on the west side of the Schuylkill, about twenty-three miles from Philadelphia. To the north-west a deep creek runs between high and rugged hills, and debouches into the Schuylkill. This stream is called the Valley Creek. A forge which was located some distance up the creek, and whose hammers were worked by the stream, is supposed to have originated the name "Valley Forge," which was afterwards applied first to the village, and then to the whole camp ground. This old forge, built previous to the Revolution, was standing there during the war. It was used for the conversion of pig iron into "blooms," and then into rod iron. This was before the day of rolling mills.

Watkins' Glen — Havana Glen — Geneva - Ithaca.

EXCURSION No. 30.
New York to Watkins' Glen and return.

	MILES.
New York, Lake Erie and Western Railroad............to Elmira....	274
Northern Central Railway............to Watkins'....	22
Seneca Lake Steamer............to Geneva....	40
New York Central and Hudson River R. R............to Albany....	200
Day Line Hudson River Steamers............to New York....	142
Rate, - - $12.75	

EXCURSION No. 31.
New York to Watkins' Glen and return.

	MILES.
Day Line Hudson River Steamers............to Albany....	142
New York Central and Hudson River R. R............to Geneva....	200
Seneca Lake Steamer............to Watkins'....	40
Northern Central Railway............to Elmira....	22
New York, Lake Erie and Western Railroad............to New York....	274
Rate, - - $12.75	

HAVANA GLEN.

EXCURSION No. 32.
New York to Havana Glen and return.

	MILES.
New York, Lake Erie and Western Railroad............to Elmira....	274
Northern Central Railway............to Havana....	19
Northern Central Railway............to Elmira....	19
New York, Lake Erie and Western Railroad............to New York....	274
Rate, - - $11.60	

EXCURSION No. 33.
New York to Havana Glen and return.

	MILES.
New York, Lake Erie and Western Railroad............to Elmira....	274
Northern Central Railway............to Havana....	19
Northern Central Railway............to Watkins'....	3
Seneca Lake Steamer............to Geneva....	40
New York Central and Hudson River R. R............to Albany....	200
Day Line Hudson River Steamers............to New York....	142
Rate, - - $12.75	

ON THE UPPER DELAWARE.

GENEVA.

EXCURSION No. 60.
New York to Geneva and return.

		MILES
New York, Lake Erie and Western Railroad	to Elmira	274
Northern Central Railway	to Watkins	22
Seneca Lake Steamer	to Geneva	40
Seneca Lake Steamer	to Watkins	40
Northern Central Railway	to Elmira	22
New York, Lake Erie and Western Railroad	to New York	274

Rate, $13.00

ITHACA.

EXCURSION No. 95.
New York to Ithaca and return.

		MILES
New York, Lake Erie and Western Railroad	to Owego	297
Delaware, Lackawanna and Western R. R.	to Ithaca	34
Delaware, Lackawanna and Western R. R.	to Owego	35
New York, Lake Erie and Western Railroad	to New York	297

Rate, $11.75

Trouting in the Upper Delaware.

"I OWE MY GRACEFUL FIGURE TO COOLEY'S GLOBE CORSET."

COOLEY'S
CELEBRATED
Globe Corsets
MADE UNDER COOLEY'S PATENT.

Elegant, Easy, Graceful & Healthful.

SATISFACTION GUARANTEED.

Manufactur d by

Globe Manufacturing Co.
343, 345 & 347
BROADWAY,
NEW YORK.

For Sale by all First-class Dealers.

FALLS OF AWASTING

Falls of Awasting, Erie Railway.

Taughannock Falls—Clifton Springs—Chautauqua Lake.

TAUGHANNOCK FALLS.

EXCURSION No. 69.

New York to Taughannock Falls and return.

		MILES
New York, Lake Erie and Western Railroad.............	....to Owego............	237
Delaware, Lackawanna and Western R. R............	....to Ithaca............	33
Cayuga Lake Steamboat Co............	....to Taughannock......	8
Cayuga Lake Steamboat Co............	....to Ithaca............	8
Delaware, Lackawanna and Western Railroad........	....to Owego............	33
New York, Lake Erie and Western Railroad..........	....to New York.........	237

Rate, - - - $12.15

EXCURSION No. 70.

New York to Taughannock Falls and return.

		MILES
New York, Lake Erie and Western Railroad............	....to Owego............	237
Delaware, Lackawanna and Western R. R............	....to Ithaca............	33
Geneva, Ithaca and Sayre R. R............	....to Taughannock......	8
Geneva, Ithaca and Sayre R. R............	....to Ithaca............	8
Delaware, Lackawanna and Western R. R............	....to Owego............	33
New York, Lake Erie and Western Railroad............	....to New York.........	237

Rate, - - - $12.15

CLIFTON SPRINGS.

EXCURSION No. 85.

New York to Clifton Springs and return.

		MILES
Day Line Hudson River Steamers...........	....to Albany............	142
New York Central and Hudson River R. R........	....to Clifton Springs....	212
New York Central and Hudson River R. R........	....to Geneva............	12
Seneca Lake Steamer...........	....to Watkins............	40
Northern Central Railway...........	....to Elmira............	22
New York, Lake Erie and Western Railroad.......	....to New York.........	274

Rate, - - $13.25

CHAUTAUQUA LAKE.

EXCURSION No. 86.

New York to Chautauqua Lake and return.

		MILES
New York, Lake Erie and Western Railroad...........	....to Salamanca.........	414
Atlantic and Great Western Railway...........	....to Jamestown.........	34
Steamer on Chautauqua Lake...........	....to Mayville...........	22
Steamer on Chautauqua Lake...........	....to Jamestown.........	22
Atlantic and Great Western Railway...........	....to Salamanca.........	34
New York, Lake Erie and Western Railroad........	....to New York.........	414

Rate, - - - $18.00

EXCURSION No. 87.

New York to Chautauqua Lake and return.

		MILES
New York, Lake Erie and Western Railroad...........	....to Salamanca.........	414
Atlantic and Great Western Railway...........	....to Jamestown.........	34
Steamer on Chautauqua Lake...........	....to Mayville...........	22
Steamer on Chautauqua Lake...........	....to Jamestown.........	22
Buffalo and Southwestern Railroad...........	....to Buffalo............	69
New York, Lake Erie and Western Railroad...........	....to Niagara Falls......	23
New York, Lake Erie and Western Railroad (via Avon Springs or Portage).......	....to New York.........	443

Rate, - - - $19.30

CHAUTAUQUA.

View of Chautauqua—Seat of National Sunday-School Assembly.

EXCURSION No. 1.
New York to Chautauqua Lake and return.

	MILES
New York, Lake Erie and Western Railroad (via Avon Springs or Portage)	...to Niagara Falls ... 44
New York, Lake Erie and Western Railroad	..to Buffalo ... 23
Lake Shore and Michigan Southern Railway	to Brocton ... 19
Buffalo, Chautauqua Lake and Pittsburg Railway	to Mayville ... 13
Steamer on Chautauqua Lake	..to Jamestown ... 22
New York, Pennsylvania and Ohio Railroad	to Salamanca ... 51
New York, Lake Erie and Western Railroad	..to New York ... 410

Rate, $19.50

EXCURSION No. 2.
New York to Chautauqua Lake and return.

	MILES
New York, Lake Erie and Western Railroad	to Salamanca ... 414
New York, Pennsylvania and Ohio Railroad	to Jamestown ... 51
Steamer on Chautauqua Lake	to Mayville ... 22
Buffalo, Chautauqua Lake and Pittsburg Railway	to Brocton ... 13
Lake Shore and Michigan Southern Railway	to Buffalo ... 19
New York, Lake Erie and Western Railroad	to Niagara Falls ... 23
New York, Lake Erie and Western Railroad (via Avon Springs or Portage)	to New York ... 443

Rate, $19.50

EXCURSION No. 3.
New York to Chautauqua Lake and return.

	MILES
New York, Lake Erie and Western Railroad	to Salamanca ... 414
New York, Pennsylvania and Ohio Railroad	to Jamestown ... 51
Steamer on Chautauqua Lake	to Mayville ... 22
Buffalo, Chautauqua Lake and Pittsburg Railway	to Brocton ... 13
Lake Shore and Michigan Southern Railway	to Buffalo ... 49
New York, Lake Erie and Western Railroad	to Niagara Falls ... 23
New York Central and Hudson River R. R.	to Schenectady ... 280
Saratoga Div., Del. & Hud. Canal Co.'s Lines	to Saratoga ... 21
Saratoga Div., Del. & Hud. Canal Co.'s Lines	to Albany ... 38
Day Line Hudson River Steamer	to New York ... 142

Rate, $24.00

SUMMER EXCURSION ROUTES.

EXCURSION No. 79.
New York to Chautauqua Lake and return via Mauch Chunk and Philadelphia.

		MILES
New York, Lake Erie and Western Railroad *via* Avon Springs or Portage	to Niagara Falls	443
New York, Lake Erie and Western Railroad	to Buffalo	25
Lake Shore and Michigan Southern Railway	to Brocton	49
Pittsburg, Titusville and Buffalo Railway	to Mayville	14
Steamer on Chautauqua Lake	to Jamestown	22
New York, Pennsylvania and Ohio Railroad	to Salamanca	34
New York, Lake Erie and Western Railroad	to Waverly	158
Lehigh Valley Railroad	to Bethlehem	194
North Pennsylvania Railroad	to Philadelphia	55
New York and Philadelphia New Line	to New York	90

Rate, - - - $22.50

EXCURSION No. 205.
New York to Chautauqua Lake and return, via Philadelphia, to New York

		MILES
New York, Lake Erie and Western Railroad *via* Avon Springs or Portage	to Niagara Falls	443
New York, Lake Erie and Western Railroad	to Buffalo	23
Buffalo and Southwestern R. R.	to Jamestown	69
Steamer on Chautauqua Lake	to Mayville	22
Steamer on Chautauqua Lake	to Jamestown	22
New York, Pennsylvania and Ohio Railroad	to Corry	27
Pittsburg, Titusville and Buffalo Railway	to Oil City	45
Allegheny Valley Railroad	to Pittsburg	132
Pennsylvania Railroad	to Philadelphia	354
Pennsylvania Railroad	to New York	90

Rate, - $25.00

ALEXANDRIA BAY.

EXCURSION No. 38.
New York to Alexandria Bay and return.

		MILES
New York, Lake Erie and Western Railroad *via* Avon Springs or Portage	to Niagara Falls	443
New York Central and Hudson River R. R.	to Syracuse	158
Rome, Watertown and Ogdensburg R. R.	to Cape Vincent	95
Steamer	to Alexandria Bay	30
Steamer	to Cape Vincent	30
Rome, Watertown and Ogdensburg R. R.	to Syracuse	95
Syracuse, Binghamton and New York R. R.	to Binghamton	80
New York, Lake Erie and Western Railroad	to New York	215

Rate, - - $24.60

Scene near Lyndhurst

SUMMER.

Her soft descending showers
Hath April poured upon the smiling plains,
And leafy June leads on the sultry hours.
   For May hath gone,
   And Summer marches on
To take possession of his wide domains.

The skies are bright and blue,
Save where the silver clouds sail slowly by.
In every form and ever-varying hue,
   Soft breathes the gale,
   Through each sequestered vale,
And hills o'erhung with forests waving high.

   Now, in the meadows green,
The fragrant odour of the new-mown hay
Rises like incense, where the scythe hath been,
   And all the air
   Re-echoes everywhere
With sound of labour till the close of day.

   Now, hurried from the fold,
The flocks dash through the cleansing stream,
And issue dripping from the waters cold;
   Till, warm and dry,
   They all contented lie,
Shorn of their fleeces, in the sunlight's gleam.

STORIES ABOUT CURRAN.

CURRAN, the Irish barrister, was a man of great magnetic force. His oratorical powers were of the most splendid style, and his wit, pathos, and sarcasm irresistible. He is said to have received a call before he had left his bed one morning, from a man whom he had roughly, and with a good deal of insolence, cross-examined the day before.

"Sir," said this irate man, presenting himself in Curran's bedroom, and arousing the barrister from slumber to a consciousness that he was in a very awkward position, "I am the gentleman you insulted yesterday in court, in the presence of the whole county, and I have come to thrash you soundly for it." Thus suiting the action to the word, he raised a horsewhip to strike Curran, when the latter quickly said:

"You don't mean to strike a man when he's down."

"No, bedad; I'll jist wait till you've got out of bed, and then I will give it to you."

Curran's eye twinkled humorously as he replied:

"If that's the case, by George I'll lie here all day."

So amused was the Irishman at this flash of wit, that he dropped his whip, and with a hearty roar of laughter, asked Curran to shake hands with him.

His wit at times was extremely bitter, as when asked by a young poet, whom he disliked:

"Have you seen my 'Descent into Hell?'" he replied:

"No; I should be delighted to see it."

At other times his humor was warm and delightful, as for example, when his physician one morning observed:

"You seem to cough with more difficulty!" he replied:

"That is rather surprising, for I have been practicing all night."

A DEACON'S MISTAKE.

A FUNNY JOKE, and all the more palatable, as its truth can be vouched for, occurred at a prominent church in New Jersey. It seems that a worthy deacon had been very industrious in selling a new church book, costing seventy-five cents. At the service in question, the minister, just before dismissing the congregation, rose and said, "All ye who have children to baptize will please to present them next Sabbath."

The deacon, who, by the way, was a little deaf, having an eye on selling the books, and supposing the pastor was referring to them, immediately jumped up and shouted: "All you who haven't, can get as many as you want by calling on me, at seventy-five cents each."

A MAN asked for admission to a show for half price, as he had but one eye to see with.

"FREE CHOPS" is a sign hung out by a Chicago restaurant; and when the customers apply, they are shown a wood-pile and handed an axe.

"SHALL I help you over the fence?" said a polite youth to an old gentleman, who weighed 200 pounds. "Oh! no, Don't help me. You had be ter help the fence."

"WHO," said Mr. Peter Mitchell, a member of the Canadian House of Commons, to the members who were trying to choke him off— "who brayed there?" "It was an echo," retorted a member, amid a yell of delight.

HORSESHOE FALL FROM GOAT ISLAND

Niagara: The Horseshoe Fall from Goat Island.

Alexandria Bay.

EXCURSION No. 89.
New York to Alexandria Bay and return.

	MILES.
New York, Lake Erie and Western Railroad (via Avon Springs or Portage)	...to Niagara Falls..... 443
New York Central and Hudson River R. R.	......to Syracuse............ 158
Rome, Watertown and Ogdensburg R. R.	...to Cape Vincent.... 95
Steamer	...to Alexandria Bay... 30
Steamer	..to Cape Vincent.... 30
Rome, Watertown and Ogdensburg R. R.	....to Rome............ 97
New York Central and Hudson River R. R.	.....to Albany............ 110
Day Line Hudson River Steamers	....to New York...... 142

Rate, - - - $22.90

EXCURSION No. 40.
New York to Alexandria Bay and return.

	MILES.
New York, Lake Erie and Western Railroad.	....to Binghamton..... 215
Syracuse, Binghamton and New York R. R.	...to Syracuse......... 80
Rome, Watertown and Ogdensburg R. R.	..to Cape Vincent.... 95
Steamer	. to Alexandria Bay... 30
Steamer	..to Cape Vincent.... 30
Rome, Watertown and Ogdensburg R. R.	....to Rome............ 97
New York Central and Hudson River R. R.	.....to Albany............ 110
Day Line Hudson River Steamers	....to New York...... 142

Rate, - - - $17.10

EXCURSION No. 41.
New York to Alexandria Bay and return.

	MILES.
Day Line Hudson River Steamers	...to Albany.......... 142
New York Central and Hudson River R. R.	....to Rome............ 110
Rome, Watertown and Ogdensburg R. R.	...to Cape Vincent.... 97
Steamer	...to Alexandria Bay... 30
Steamer	..to Cape Vincent.... 30
Rome, Watertown and Ogdensburg R. R.	...to Syracuse......... 95
Syracuse, Binghamton and New York R. R.	....to Binghamton..... 80
New York, Lake Erie and Western Railroad	...to New York...... 215

Rate, - - - $17.10

EXCURSION No. 42.
New York to Alexandria Bay and return.

	MILES.
New York, Lake Erie and Western Railroad (via Avon Springs or Portage)	...to Niagara Falls..... 443
New York Central and Hudson River R. R.	....to Lewistown....... 7
Steamer	...to Toronto........ 36
Royal Mail Line Steamers	..to Alexandria Bay... 235
Steamer	...to Clayton.......... 12
Utica and Black River R. R. (via Trenton Falls)	...to Utica............ 108
New York Central and Hudson River R. R.	...to Albany........... 95
Day Line Hudson River Steamers	....to New York...... 142

Rate, - - - $24.10

EXCURSION No. 43.
New York to Alexandria Bay and return.

	MILES.
New York, Lake Erie and Western Railroad	...to Binghamton..... 215
Delaware, Lackawanna and Western Railroad	...to Utica........... 95
Utica and Black River R. R. (via Trenton Falls)	...to Clayton........ 108
Steamer	...to Alexandria Bay... 12
Steamer	...to Clayton.......... 12
Utica & Black River R. R. (via Trenton Falls)	...to Utica........... 108
New York Central and Hudson River R. R.	...to Albany........... 95
Day Line Hudson River Steamers	....to New York...... 142

Rate, - - - $17.45

THE GLADNESS OF NATURE.

There are notes of joy from the hang-bird and wren,
　And the gossip of swallows through all the sky;
The ground-squirrel gaily chirps by his den,
　And the wilding-bee hums merrily by.

The clouds are at play in the azure space,
　And their shadows at play on the bright green vale,
And here they stretch to the frolic chase,
　And there they roll on the easy gale.

There's a dance of leaves in that aspen bower,
　There's a titter of winds in that beechen tree;
There's a smile on the fruit, and a smile on the flower,
　And a laugh from the brook that runs to the sea.

And look at the broad-faced sun, how he smiles
　On the dewy earth that smiles in his ray,
On the leaping waters and gay young isles;
　Ay, look, and he'll smile thy gloom away!

Alexandria Bay Montreal.

EXCURSION No. 72.
New York to Alexandria Bay and return.

		MILES
New York, Lake Erie and Western Railroad (via Avon Springs or Portage)	to Niagara Falls	443
New York Central and Hudson River R. R.	to Utica	211
Utica and Black River R. R. (via Trenton Falls)	to Clayton	108
Steamer	to Alexandria Bay	12
Steamer	to Clayton	12
Utica and Black River R. R. (via Trenton Falls)	to Utica	108
Delaware, Lackawanna and Western R. R.	to Binghamton	95
New York, Lake Erie and Western Railroad	to New York	215

Rate, - - - $26.00

EXCURSION No. 73.
New York to Alexandria Bay and return.

		MILES
New York, Lake Erie and Western Railroad (via Avon Springs or Portage)	to Niagara Falls	443
New York Central and Hudson River R. R.	to Utica	211
Utica and Black River R. R. (via Trenton Falls)	to Clayton	108
Steamer	to Alexandria Bay	12
Steamer	to Clayton	12
Utica and Black River R. R. (via Trenton Falls)	to Utica	108
New York Central and Hudson River R. R.	to Albany	95
Day Line Hudson River Steamers	to New York	142

Rate, - - - $23.75

MONTREAL.

EXCURSION No. 44.
New York to Montreal and Return.

		MILES
New York, Lake Erie and Western Railroad (via Avon Springs or Portage)	to Niagara Falls	443
New York Central and Hudson River R. R.	to Syracuse	158
Rome, Watertown and Ogdensburg R. R.	to Cape Vincent	95
Steamer	to Alexandria Bay	30
Royal Mail Line Steamers	to Montreal	165
Grand Trunk Railway	to Rouse's Point	50
Champlain Division D. & H. C. Co's Lines	to Plattsburg	23
Champlain Division D. & H. C. Co's Lines or Lake Champlain Steamers	to Ft. Ticonderoga	68
Saratoga Div., Del. & Hud. C. Co's Lines	to Baldwin	5
Lake George Steamer	to Caldwell	36
Stage	to Glen's Falls	9
Saratoga Div., Del. & Hud. C. Co's Lines	to Saratoga	23
Saratoga Div., Del. & Hud. C. Co's Lines	to Albany	38
Day Line Hudson River Steamers	to New York	142

Rate, - - - $34.50

EXCURSION No. 45.
New York to Montreal and return.

		MILES
New York, Lake Erie and Western Railroad	to Binghamton	215
Delaware, Lackawanna and Western R. R.	to Utica	95
Utica and Black River R. R. (via Trenton Falls)	to Clayton	108
Steamer	to Alexandria Bay	12
Royal Mail Line Steamer	to Montreal	165
Grand Trunk Railway	to Rouse's Point	50
Champlain Division. D. & H. C. Co's Lines	to Plattsburg	23
Champlain Division. D. & H. Canal Co's Lines or Lake Champlain Ste.	to Ft. Ticonderoga	68
Saratoga Div., Del. & Hud. C. Co's Lines	to Saratoga	61
Saratoga Div., Del. & Hud. C. Co's Lines	to Albany	38
Day Line Hudson River Steamers	to New York	142

Rate, - - - $27.00

SAM'S LETTER.

I WONDER who the d-d-devil w-wote me thth letter. I thuppoth the b-heth way to f-find out ith to open it and thee. (*Opens letter.*) Thome lun-lunatic hath w-witten me thth letter. He hath w-witten it upthide down. I wonder if he th-thought I wath going to w-wead it thanding on my head. Oh, yeth, I thee; I had it t-t-turned upthide down. "Amewica!" Who the d-devil do I know in Amewica? I am glad he hath g-given me hith addweth anyhow. Oh, yeth, I thee, it ith from Tham. I alwayth know Tham'th handwiting when I thee hith name at the b-bottom of it. Tham alwayth wath an ath; but you'd like him. "My dear bwother—" Tham alwayth called me bwother. I-I thuppoth ith becauth hith m-mother and my mother wath the thame woman, and we never had any thith-terth. When we were boyth we were lalth together. The uth to ge-get off a pwoverb when they thaw uth com-coming down the stweet. It ith vewy good if I could only think of it. I can never wecollect anything that I can't we-member. Ith—it ith the early bir-bird ith the early bir-bird that knoweth ith own father. Whht non-nonthenth that ith! How co-could a bir-bird know ith own father? Ith a withe—ith a withe child—ith the withe child that geth the wom. T-thath not wite. What non-nonthenth that ith! No pa-pawent would allow hith child to ga-gather woms. Ith a whyme. Ith fish of-of a feather. Fish of a fea— What non-non-thenth! For fish don'th have featherth. Ith bir-birdth—ith b-birdth of a feather—b-birdth of a-of a feather flock together. B-birdth of a feather! Juth ath if a who-who-whole flock of b-birdth had only one f-feather! They'd all catch cold, and only one b-bird e-could have that f-feather, and he'd fly sidewithe. What con-confounded nonthenth that ith! Flock to-together! Of courth th-they'd flock together. Who ever her-heard of a bird being such a durned f-fool ath to g-go into a e-corner and flo-flock by himthelf? "I wo-wote you a letter thome time ago—" Thath a lie; he d-did't wi-wite me a letter. If he had witten me a letter he would have pothed it, and I would have g-got it; tho, of courth, he didn't poth it, and then he didn't wite it. Thath eathy. Oh, yeth, I thee: "but I dwopped it into the poht-office forgetting to diweet it." Tham alwayth wath an ath. I wonder who the d-die-dickenth got that letter. I wonder if the poth-pothman ith gwoin' awound inquiwing for a f-fellow without a name. I wonder if there ith a f-fellow without any name. If there ith any f-fellow without any name, how the d-devil doeth he who he ith him-thelf? I—I wonder if thuch a fellow could get mawied. How could he uk hith wife to take hith name if he h-had no name?. Thath one of thothe thingth no fellow can f-find out. "I have juth made a thartling discovery." Tham'th alwayth d-doing thomthing. "I have dithcovered that my mother ith—that m-my mother ith not my m-mother; that a—the old nurth is my m-mother, and that you are not my b-bwother, and a—tha-that I wath changed at my birth." How c-can a fellow be changed at hith b-birth? If he ith not himthelf, who the de-de-devil ith he? If Tham'th m-mother is not hith m-mother, and the nurth is hith mother, and Tham ithn't my bwother, who the d-devil am I? That'h one of thothe thingth that no fel-fellow can find out. "I have p-purchathed an ethtate thome-thome-where—" Dothn't the id-idiot know wh-where h-he hath bought it? Oh, yeth: "on the b-bankth of the M-M-Mithithippi." Wh-who the d-devil ith M-Mithithippi? I g-gueth ith Tham'th m-mother-in-law. Tham'th got mawied. He th-thayth he felt v-vewy ner-nervouth. Any fel-fellow feelth nervouth when h-he knoweth he ith go-going to make an ath of himthelf. Tham'th got a mother-in-law. He alwayth wath a lucky fellow getting th-thingth he didn't want, and hadn't any uth for. Thpeaking of mother-in-lawth. I had a fwiend who had a mother-in-law, and he didn't like her pwetty well; and she f-felt the thame way toward him; and they went away on a th-theamer acwoth the ocean, and they got wecked, catht away on a waft, and they floated awound with their feet in the water and other amuthethment, living on thuch thingth ath they could pick up—thardinth, ithewcam, owangeth, and other e-canned goodth that were floating awound. When that wath all gone, everybody ate everybody elth. F-finally only himthelf and hith mother-in-law wath left, and they pl-played a game of e-eardth to thee who thould be eaten up—himthelf or hith mother-in law. A-a—the mother-in-lawlotht. H-he treated her handthomely, only he thrapped h-her flat on her back, and e-carved her gently. H-h-he thayth that wath the f-firth time that he ever weally enjoyed a m-mother-in-law.—*Lord Dundreary.*

The Leading Hotel of the City, and only one with Elevator.

OSBURN HOUSE,

Rochester, N. Y.

GEO. A. BUCK. WM. H. SANGER

THE EBBITT HOUSE,
WASHINGTON, D. C.

Board and Room at $3.00 and $4.00 per day. Parlor and Alcove Rooms at equally low rates. Bull's Eyes, or Top Floor (nice rooms) at $2.50 per day. The Clergy have always been received at a Liberal Discount. Army and Navy Officers at special rates.

☞ *Four Iron Fire Escapes. Splendid New Hydraulic Elevator, Otis, Bro. & Co.'s favorite and best job.* ☜

Special attention paid to persons going to and returning from Florida.

C. C. WILLARD, Proprietor.

A Railroad in the Clouds, Erie Switchback Route. (see page 14).

Montreal.

EXCURSION No. 46.
New York to Montreal and return.

		MILES.
New York, Lake Erie and Western Railroad	to Binghamton	215
Delaware, Lackawanna and Western R. R.	to Utica	95
Utica and Black River R. R. (via Trenton Falls)	to Clayton	108
Steamer	to Alexandria Bay	12
Royal Mail Line Steamers	to Montreal	165
Grand Trunk Railway	to Rouse's Point	50
Champlain Division, D. & H. C. Co's Lines	to Plattsburg	23
Champlain Division, D. & H. C. Co's Lines or Lake Champlain Steamer	to Ft. Ticonderoga	68
Saratoga Division, Del. and Hud. C. Co's Lines	to Baldwin	5
Lake George Steamer	to Caldwell	36
Stage	to Glen's Falls	9
Saratoga Division, Del. and Hud. C. Co's Lines	to Saratoga	23
Saratoga Division, Del. and Hud. C. Co's Lines	to Albany	38
Day Line Hudson River Steamers	to New York	142

Rate, - - - - $29.50

EXCURSION No. 47.
New York to Montreal and return.

		MILES.
New York, Lake Erie and Western Railroad	to Binghamton	215
Susquehanna Div., Del. & Hud. C. Co's Lines	to Junction	67
Cooperstown and Susquehanna Valley Railroad	to Cooperstown	16
Otsego Lake Steamer and Stage	to Richfield Springs	16
Delaware, Lackawanna and Western Railroad	to Utica	85
Utica and Black River R. R. (via Trenton Falls)	to Clayton	108
Steamer	to Alexandria Bay	12
Royal Mail Line Steamers	to Montreal	165
Grand Trunk Railway	to Rouse's Point	50
Champlain Division, D. & H. C. Co's Lines	to Plattsburg	23
Champlain Division, D. & H. C. Co's Lines or Lake Champlain Steamer	to Ft. Ticonderoga	68
Saratoga Division, Del. & Hud. C. Co's Lines	to Saratoga	61
Saratoga Division, Del. & Hud. C. Co's Lines	to Albany	38
Day Line Hudson River Steamers	to New York	142

Rate, - - - - $28.75

EXCURSION No. 48.
New York to Montreal and return.

		MILES.
New York, Lake Erie and Western Railroad	to Binghamton	215
Susquehanna Div., Del. & Hud. C. Co's Lines	to Junction	67
Cooperstown and Susquehanna Valley R. R.	to Cooperstown	16
Otsego Lake Steamer and Stage	to Richfield Springs	16
Delaware, Lackawanna and Western R. R.	to Utica	85
Utica and Black River R. R. (via Trenton Falls)	to Clayton	108
Steamer	to Alexandria Bay	12
Royal Mail Line Steamers	to Montreal	165
Grand Trunk Railway	to Rouse's Point	50
Champlain Divison, D. & H. C. Co's Lines	to Plattsburgh	23
Champlain Division, D. & H. C. Co's Lines or Lake Champlain Steamer	to Ft. Ticonderoga	68
Saratoga Div., Del. & Hud. C. Co's Lines	to Baldwin	5
Lake George Steamer	to Caldwell	36
Stage	to Glen's Falls	9
Saratoga Div., Del. & Hud. C. Co's Lines	to Saratoga	23
Saratoga Div., Del. & Hud. C. Co's Lines	to Albany	38
Day Line Hudson River Steamers	to New York	142

Rate, - - - - $31.25

EXCURSION No. 49.
New York to Montreal and return.

		MILES.
New York, Lake Erie and Western Railroad (via Avon Springs or Portage)	to Niagara Falls	443
New York Central and Hudson River R. R.	to Utica	211
Utica and Black River R. R. (via Trenton Falls)	to Clayton	108
Steamer	to Alexandria Bay	12
Royal Mail Line Steamers	to Montreal	165
Grand Trunk Railway	to Rouse's Point	50
Champlain Divison, D. & H. C. Co's Lines	to Plattsburgh	23
Champlain Division, D. & H. C. Co's Lines or Lake Champlain Steamer	to Ft. Ticonderoga	68
Saratoga Div., Del. & Hud. C. Co's Lines	to Baldwin	5
Lake George Steamer	to Caldwell	36
Stage	to Glen's Falls	9
Saratoga Div., Del. C. Co's Lines	to Saratoga	23
Saratoga Div., Del. & Hud. C. Co's Lines	to Albany	38
Day Line Hudson River Steamers	to New York	142

Rate, - - - - $34.30

THERE'S ROOM AT THE TOP.

They say the professions are crowded
  By seekers for fame and for bread;
That their members are pushing each other
  As close as their footsteps can tread.
But be not discouraged, my brother,
  Nor suffer exertion to stop.
Though thousands are pressing around you,
  There is plenty of room at the top.

Be true to thy love and thy country
  The dastard wins never a prize;
But the earnest are ever the victors,
  And he who on justice relies,
Who wins the good guerdon by labor,
  Will garner sweet rest as his crop,
And find, as the hills sink below him,
  That there's room enough at the top.

Oh! let not the evil disturb you,
  There's good if you but search it out;
Make pure thine own conscience, my brother,
  Nor mind what the rest are about.
And whether your work may have fallen
  In sanctum, or office, or shop,
Remember the low grounds are crowded,
  But there's always room at the top.

THE SHIP OF FAITH.

A CERTAIN colored brother had been holding forth to his little flock upon the ever fruitful topic of Faith, and he closed his exhortation above as follows:

My bruddren, ef yous gwine to git saved, you got to git on board de Ship ob Faith. I tell you, my bruddren, dere ain't no odder way. Dere ain't no gitting up de back stairs, nor goin' 'cross lots; you can't do dat way, my bruddren, you got to git on board de Ship of Faith. Once 'pon a time dere was a lot of colored people, an' dey was all gwine to de promised land. Well, dey knowed dere want no odder way for 'em to do but to git on board de Ship of Faith. So dey all went down an' got on board, de ole gran faders, an' de ole granmudders, an' de pickaninnies, and all de res' ob 'em. Dey all got on board 'ceptin' one mons'us big feller, he said he's gwine to swim, he was. "W'y?" dey said, "you can't swim so fur like dat. It am a powerful long way to de promised land!" He said, "I kin swim anywhur, I kin. I git board no boat, no, 'deed!" Well, my bruddren, all dey could say to dat poor disluded man dey couldn't git him on board de Ship of Faith, so dey started off. De day was fair, de win' right; de sun shinin' and ev'ryt'ing b'utibul, an' dis big feller he pull off his close and plunge in de water. Well, he was a powerful swimmer, dat man, 'deed he war; he war dat powerful he kep' right 'long side de boat all de time; he kep' a hollerin' out to de people on de boat, sayin': "What you doin' dere, you folks, brillin' in de sun; you better come down heah in de water, nice an' cool down here." But dey said: "Man alive, you better come up here in dis boat while you got a chance." But he said, "No, indeedy! I git aboard no boat. I'm havin' plenty fun in de water." Well, bimeby, my bruddren, what do you tink dat pore man seen? A horrible, awful shock, my bruddren; mouf wide open, teef more'n a foot long, ready to chaw dat pore man all up de minute he catch him. Well, when he seen dat shark he begun to git awful scared, an' he holler out to de folks on board de ship: "Take me on board, take me on board, quick!" But dey say: "No, indeed; you wouldn't come up here when you had an invite, you got to swim now."

He look over his shoulder an' he seen dat shark a-comin', an' he let hisself out. Fust it was de man an' den it was de shark, an' den it was de man again, dat away, my brudder, plum to de promised land. Dat am de blessed troof I'm a tellin' you dis minute. What do you t'ink was awaitin' for him on de odder shore when he got dere? A horrible, awful lion, my bruddren, was a-stan'in' dere on de shore, a-lashin' his sides wid his tail, an' a-roarin' away fit to devour dat poor nigger de minit he git on de shore. Well he war powerful scared den, he don't know what he gwine to do. If he stay in de water de shark eat him up; if he go on de shore de lion eat him up; he dunno what to do. But he put his trust in de Lord, an' went for de shore. Dat lion he give a fearful roar an' bound for him; but, my bruddren, as sure as you 'live an' breeve, dat horrible awful lion he jumped clean ober dat pore feller's head in de water; an' de shark eat de lion. But, my bruddren, don't put your trust in such circumstance; dat pore man he done git saved, but I tell you de Lord ain't a gwine to furnish a lion for every nigger!

A COUNTRYMAN traveling in a street car, pulled the bell strap vigorously, and made the bell ring at each end. "What are you ringing at both ends for?" said the conductor; "Because I wish the thing to stop at both ends."

Montreal.

EXCURSION No. 74.
New York to Montreal and return.

		MILES.
New York, Lake Erie and Western Railroad (via Avon Springs or Portage)	...to Niagara Falls	443
New York Central and Hudson River R. R.	...to Utica	211
Utica and Black River R. R. (via Trenton Falls)	...to Clayton	108
Steamer	...to Alexandria Bay	12
Steamer	...to Ogdensburg	35
Ferry	...to Prescott	1
St. Lawrence and Ottawa Railway	...to Ottawa	54
Ottawa River Navigation Co's Steamers	...to Montreal	125
Grand Trunk Railway	...to Rouse's Point	50
Champlain Division, Del. & Hud. Canal Co's Lines	...to Plattsburgh	23
Champlain Division, Del. & Hud. Canal Co's Lines, or Lake Champlain Steamer	...to Ft. Ticonderoga	68
Saratoga Division, Del. & Hud. Canal Co's Lines	...to Baldwin	5
Lake George Steamer	...to Caldwell	36
Stage	...to Glen's Falls	9
Saratoga Division, Del. & Hud. Canal Co's Lines	...to Saratoga	28
Saratoga Division, Del. & Hud. Canal Co's Lines	...to Albany	38
Day Line Hudson River Steamers	...to New York	142

Rate, - - - - $33.50

EXCURSION No. 75.
New York to Montreal and return.

		MILES.
New York, Lake Erie and Western Railroad	...to Binghamton	415
Delaware, Lackawanna and Western R. R.	...to Utica	95
Utica and Black River R. R. (via Trenton Falls	...to Clayton	108
Steamer	...to Alexandria Bay	12
Steamer	...to Morristown	20
Ferry	...to Brockville	1
Canada Central Railway	...to Ottawa	76
Ottawa River Navigation Co's Steamers	...to Montreal	125
Grand Trunk Railway	...to Rouse's Point	50
Champlain Division, Del. & Hud. C. Co's Lines	...to Plattsburgh	23
Champlain Division, Del. & Hud. C. Co's Lines or Lake Champlain Steamer	...to Ft. Ticonderoga	68
Saratoga Division, Del. & Hud. C. Co's Lines	...to Saratoga	61
Saratoga Division, Del. & Hud. C. Co's Lines	...to Albany	38
Day Line Hudson River Steamers	...to New York	142

Rate, - - - - $26.00

EXCURSION K. X. 19.
New York to Montreal and return.

		MILES.
New York, Lake Erie and Western Railroad (via Avon Springs or Portage)	...to Niagara Falls	443
New York Central and Hudson River R. R.	...to Lewiston	7
Steamer	...to Toronto	36
Grand Trunk Railway or Royal Mail Line Steamers	...to Montreal	333
Grand Trunk Railway	...to Rouse's Point	50
Champlain Div., D. & H. Canal Co's Lines	...to Plattsburg	23
Champlain Div., D. & H. Canal Co's Lines or Lake Champlain Steamer	...to Ft. Ticonderoga	68
Saratoga Division, D. & H. Canal Co's Lines	...to Baldwin	5
Lake George Steamer	...to Caldwell	36
Stage	...to Glen's Falls	9
Saratoga Division, D. & H. Canal Co's Lines	...to Saratoga	23
Saratoga Division, D. & H. Canal Co's Lines	to Troy	32
New York Central and Hudson River R. R.	...to New York	148

Rate, - - - - $35.50

EXCURSION K. X. 20.
New York to Montreal and return.

		MILES.
New York, Lake Erie and Western Railroad (via Avon Springs or Portage)	...to Niagara Falls	443
New York Central and Hudson River R. R.	...to Lewiston	7
Steamer	...to Toronto	36
Grand Trunk Railway or Royal Mail Line Steamers	...to Montreal	333
Grand Trunk Railway	...to Rouse's Point	50
Champlain Div., D. & H. Canal Co's Lines	...to Plattsburg	23
Champlain Div., D. & H. Canal Co's Lines or Lake Champlain Steamer	...to Ft. Ticonderoga	68
Saratoga Division	...to Baldwin	5
Lake George Steamer	...to Caldwell	36
Stage	...to Glen's Falls	9
Saratoga Division, D. & H. Canal Co's Lines	...to Saratoga	23
Saratoga Division, D. & H. Canal Co's Lines	...to Albany	38
People's (Night) Line Hudson River Steamers	...to New York	142

Rate, - - - - $34.00

EPITAPHS.

In Cape May Cemetery, is a stone erected to the memory of

"MARY JANE,
Aged 11 years and 8 months.

"She was not smart, she was not fair,
But hearts with grief for her are swellin'
And empty stands her little chair
She died of eatin' watermelon."

Near San Diego, California, a tombstone inscription thus reads:

"This yere is sakrid to the memory of William Henry Skutaken, who caim to his death by bein shot by Colt's revolver one of the old kind, brass mounted and of such is the kingdom of heaven."

A tombstone in Iowa (Burlington) has this stanza:

"Beneath this stone our baby lays,
He neither cries nor hollers;
He lived just one and twenty days,
And cost us forty dollars."

The following lines are appropriate enough on the tombstone of one who had lead a selfish and useless life:

"Here lies a man who did no good,
And if he'd lived he never would;
Where he's gone or how he fares,
Nobody knows & nobody cares."

Over the remains of one Thomas Woodcock are these lines:

"Here lies the remains of Thomas Woodhen,
The most amiable of husbands, and excellent of men."

"N. B.—His real name was Woodcock, but it wouldn't rhyme. *His Widow.*"

An inscription on a tombstone in East Tennessee concluded thus:

"She lived a life of virtue and died of the cholera morbus, caused by eating green fruit, in the hope of a blessed immortality, at the early age of 21 years, 7 months and 16 days. Reader, go thou and do likewise."

AN ACTOR'S TRIUMPH.

GREAT effects upon the stage are produced only by great preparation. When Charlotte Cushman played the part of *Meg Merrilies*, and Jefferson enacts the part of *Rip Van Winkle*, and Sothern produces *Lord Dundreary*, our delight and satisfaction are the result of a profound and untiring application of the actor to study of the art; and no man or woman can hold audiences for a lifetime without that preparation which great artists always give to great conceptions. There was once an English actor so terribly in earnest with the study of his profession, that he made a mark on his generation never exceeded by any other tragedian! He was a little, dark man, with a voice naturally harsh, but he determined, when comparatively young, to play the character of *Sir Giles Overreach*, in Massinger's drama, as no other man ever played it before. He resolved to give years of indefatigable industry in preparing himself for the part, and to devote his whole intellect to a proper conception of the character. In the whole range of English dramatic literature, the character of *Sir Giles* is estimated one of the greatest pieces of effective villany and untamable passion ever portrayed, and little Edmund Kean set himself to the task of producing on the London stage all the effect which the author intended. With what intensity he studied the language, how he flung himself, with a kind of rage, into the feeling of the piece, all his biographers have recorded. His wife said that he would often remain up all night before the pier-glass, endeavoring to realize, by gesture, modulation and action, the conception at which he had arrived. At last, after repeated refusals of the management to appear as *Sir Giles*, saying he was not ready yet, and must still give more time to the rehearsal, he consented to have the play announced, as now he felt he could do it justice. And what was the effect of all this hard work and unceasing study of the part? Fortunately we know all about it, although Kean played it on that memorable evening more than fifty years ago. It was one of the grandest effects ever witnessed on the English stage. We have accounts from various eye-witnesses of the sensation and the enthusiasm the presentation of this character produced, when Kean, full ripe for the occasion, came upon the stage as *Sir Giles*; and some of the triumphs of that wonderful evening in 1861, at Drury Lane, are well known. It was observed that when he walked in from the wings there was that in his burning eye which betokened greater determination than usual, and Lord Byron, who was in a stage-box, whispered to the poet Moore, that something dreadful was written on the great actor's countenance, something more suggestive of power even than he had ever noticed before. And never till then, in the history of the stage, was there witnessed such an exhibition of forceful endeavor.

Throughout the whole play Kean bore himself like a fury; but it was reserved for the last scene to stamp an impression which existed during the lifetime of all who were present. The great actor himself shook like a strong oak in the whirlwind of his passionate vengeance, as displayed in the closing sentences of the play, and when he was removed from the stage, his face, turned to the spectators, was so awful, that Byron was seized with a convulsive fit, and fell forward pale as death itself. The solemn stillness of the house was broken by screams of terror from boxes and gallery; the pit rose *en masse.* Mrs. Glover, an actress of long experience and great talent, fainted outright on the stage; Mrs. Horn, who was also playing in the piece, staggered to a chair and wept aloud at the appalling sight of Kean's agony and rage. Munden, a veteran on the boards, who played the part of *Marall*, stood so transfixed with astonishment and terror that he had to be carried off from the scene by main force, his eyes riveted on Kean's convulsive and awful countenance. The actor that night was master of the situation, and profound and earnest study gave him the clue to his great achievement.

GIBSON HOUSE,
Fourth and Walnut Streets,

O. H. GEFFROY.
WM. GIBSON.

CINCINNATI, OHIO.

CARROLLTON HOTEL,
BALTIMORE, LIGHT and GERMAN STS.
BALTIMORE, MD.

RATES REDUCED TO $3.00 AND $2.50 PER DAY.
ACCORDING TO LOCATION OF ROOMS.

The most convenient and latest built Hotel in the city. Elevator runs continuously to all floors. All lines of city passenger cars pass its doors.

F. W. COLEMAN, MANAGER.

NIAGARA FALLS.

YOUR journey is completed. You are at Niagara. You have traversed the entire length of the Erie Railway between New York and Niagara Falls, 444 miles, by daylight; have passed through the beautiful valley of the Passaic; through the historic region of the Ramapo and the rich dairy lands of Orange county; have crossed the Shawangunk range of mountains; been spellbound by the thrilling and interesting scenes of the upper Delaware region; have followed the meanderings of the Susquehanna, Chemung and Canisteo Rivers; have witnessed the rapids and falls of the Genesee River, and now to crown all, you are face to face with the Falls of Niagara, commanding the most intense and awe-inspiring admiration of the observer. Although our artist has skillfully portrayed in the accompanying cut one of the principal features of this great wonder of Nature, no representation or description can convey an adequate idea of the sublimity of the scene. The eye must see the great volume of rushing waters tearing over the rocks and hurrying madly toward the precipice, over which they plunge into the seething basin of the Niagara, one hundred and sixty feet below; and the ear must hear the tremendous roar of the cataract, mingled as it is with the voice of the great Architect, in order to appreciate Niagara.

Montreal.

EXCURSION K. X. 21.
New York to Montreal and return.

		MILES.
New York, Lake Erie and Western Railroad (via Avon Springs or Portage)	....to Niagara Falls	443
New York Central and Hudson River R. R.	....to Lewiston	7
Steamer	....to Toronto	36
Grand Trunk Railway or Royal Mail Line Steamers	....to Montreal	333
Grand Trunk Railway	....to Rouse's Point	50
Champlain Div., Del. & Hud. Canal Co's Lines	....to Plattsburgh	23
Champlain Division, Del. & Hud. Canal Co's Lines or Lake Champlain Steamer	....to Ft. Ticonderoga	68
Saratoga Division, Del. & Hud. Canal Co's Lines	....to Saratoga	61
Saratoga Division, Del. & Hud. Canal Co's Lines	....to Troy	32
New York Central and Hudson River Railroad	....to New York	148

Rate, - - - - $31.50

EXCURSION K. X. 22.
New York to Montreal and return.

		MILES.
New York, Lake Erie and Western Railway (via Avon Springs or Portage)	....to Niagara Falls	443
New York Central and Hudson River R. R.	....to Lewiston	7
Steamer	....to Toronto	36
Grand Trunk Railway or Royal Mail Line Steamers	....to Montreal	333
Grand Trunk Railway	....to Rouse's Point	50
Champlain Division, Del. & Hud. C. Co's Lines	....to Plattsburgh	23
Champlain Division, Del. & Hud. C. Co's Lines or Lake Champlain Steamer	....to Ft. Ticonderoga	68
Saratoga Division, Del. & Hud. C. Co's Lines	....to Saratoga	61
Saratoga Division, Del. & Hud. C. Co's Lines	....to Albany	38
People's (Night) Line Hudson River Steamers	....to New York	142

Rate - - - - $30.00

EXCURSION K. X. 26.
New York to Montreal and return.

		MILES.
New York, Lake Erie and Western Railroad (via Avon Springs or Portage)	....to Niagara Falls	443
New York Central and Hudson River R. R.	....to Lewiston	7
Steamer	....to Toronto	36
Grand Trunk Railway or Royal Mail Line Steamers	....to Montreal	333
Grand Trunk Railway	....to Rouse's Point	50
Champlain Division, Del. & Hud. C. Co's Lines	....to Plattsburgh	23
Champlain Division, Del. & Hud. C. Co's Lines or Lake Champlain Steamer	....to Ft. Ticonderoga	68
Saratoga Division, Del. & Hud. C. Co's Lines	....to Baldwin	5
Lake George Steamer	....to Caldwell	36
Stage	....to Glen's Falls	9
Saratoga Division, Del. & Hud. C. Co's Lines	....to Saratoga	23
Saratoga Division, Del. & Hud. C. Co's Lines	....to Albany	38
Day Line Hudson River Steamers	....to New York	142

Rate, - - - $34.50

EXCURSION K. X. 27.
New York to Montreal and return.

		MILES.
New York, Lake Erie and Western Railroad (via Avon Springs or Portage)	....to Niagara Falls	443
New York Central and Hudson River R. R.	....to Lewiston	7
Steamer	....to Toronto	36
Grand Trunk Railway or Royal Mail Line Steamers	....to Montreal	333
Grand Trunk Railway	....to Rouse's Point	50
Champlain Division, Del. & Hud. C. Co's Lines	....to Plattsburgh	23
Champlain Division, Del. & Hud. C. Co's Lines or Lake Champlain Steamer	....to Ft. Ticonderoga	68
Saratoga Division, Del. & Hud. C. Co's Lines	....to Saratoga	61
Saratoga Division, Del. & Hud. C. Co's Lines	....to Albany	38
Day Line Hudson River Steamers	....to New York	142

Rate, - - - $30.50

NIAGARA FALLS.

The Niagara River, the strait or link connecting the two great lakes, Erie and Ontario, though but thirty-four miles long, yet passes in that brief space through a tremendous struggle with the rock-ribbed battlements which line and traverse its current. In those thirty-four miles it accomplishes a total descent of three hundred and thirty-four feet, fifty-one feet of which it descends in the space of three quarters of a mile in the Rapids which mark its approach to the terrible leap of nearly two hundred feet more the world renowned Falls of Niagara.

Over this great cataract has been pouring ceaselessly through the centuries of the past, with a deafening roar of a thousand thunders, a torrent of water three-fourths of a mile wide and twenty feet in depth, or an aggregate, it is calculated, of a hundred millions of tons per hour. No wonder that to this grandest of natural shrines the untutored aborigines were wont to come yearly to worship their Great Spirit and propitiate him by the sacrifice of an Indian maiden, sent down on the current in a flower-laden canoe to her death in the terrible vortex; no wonder that they led thither the first missionaries who penetrated these wilds and pointed in speechless awe to the mighty cataract; and no wonder that in these later days thousands and thousands of tourists from every part of this country and Europe annually make this spot their destination, and stand gazing in mute surprise, as did the savage and the priest before them, at this wonder of the world.

From the American side of the Falls the visitor has access to the various rocky islands— Goat, Chapin's, Luna and the Three Sisters—which break the face of the Falls and enable him to overlook its very brink midway in the river's current. From this side, too, he descends to the Cave of the Winds, and may visit the Whirlpool, Chasm Tower and the Devil's Hole.

From the Canada side, opposite, which is reached by a wire suspension bridge 1268 feet long, may be viewed the magnificent sweep of the cataract known as the Horseshoe Fall 1900 feet across, the Burning Spring, the historic village of Chippewa and the battle field of Lundy's Lane. Or, by a railroad running on an inclined plane, from a point on the American side near the brink of the cataract, the visitor may descend to the river directly below the Falls, and looking upward at them from the deck of the ferry-boat which plies from shore to shore, may more than before realize the immensity and grandeur of the scene. It will leave in his memory an impression and sense of admiration that a life-time will not serve to eradicate.

Further on we purpose to illustrate other scenes and places of note along the line of this celebrated road.

SUMMER EXCURSION ROUTES.

Montreal—Quebec.

EXCURSION K. N. 185.
New York to Montreal and return.

	MILES
New York, Lake Erie and Western Railroad via Avon Springs or Portage	to Niagara Falls ... 115
New York Central and Hudson River Railroad	to Lewiston ... 7
Steamer	to Toronto ... 36
Grand Trunk Railway or Royal Mail Line Steamers	to Montreal ... 333
Grand Trunk Railway	to Rouse's Point ... 50
Champlain Division, Del. & Hud. C. Co's Lin. s	to Plattsburgh ... 23
Lake Champlain Steamer	to Burlington ... 25
Central Vermont Railroad	to South Vernon ... 178
Connecticut River Railroad	to Springfield ... 50
New York, New Haven and Hartford R. R.	to New York ... 136

Rate, $33.25

QUEBEC.

EXCURSION K. N. 16
New York to Quebec and return.

	MILES
New York, Lake Erie and Western Railroad via Avon Springs or Portage	to Niagara Falls ... 115
New York Central and Hudson River R. R.	to Lewiston ... 7
Steamer	to Toronto ... 36
Grand Trunk Railway or Royal Mail Line Steamers	to Montreal ... 333
Grand Trunk Railway or Royal Mail Line Steamers	to Quebec ... 172
Grand Trunk Railway	to Sherbrooke ... 121
Passumpsic Railroad	to White Riv. June ... 115
Central Vermont Railroad	to South Vernon ... 74
Connecticut River Railroad	to Springfield ... 50
New York, New Haven and Hartford R. R.	to New York ... 136

Rate, $34.50

EXCURSION K. N. 188
New York to Quebec and return.

	MILES
New York, Lake Erie and Western Railroad via Avon Springs or Portage	to Niagara Falls ... 115
New York Central and Hudson River R. R.	to Lewiston ... 7
Steamer	to Toronto ... 33
Grand Trunk Railway or Royal Mail Line Steamers	to Montreal ... 333
Grand Trunk Railway or Royal Mail Line Steamers	to Quebec ... 172
Grand Trunk Railway	to Sherbrooke ... 121
Passumpsic Railroad	to Wells River ... 105
Montpelier and Wells River Railroad	to Montpelier ... 38
Central Vermont Railroad	to Burlington ... 41
Lake Champlain Steamers	to Ft. Ticonderoga ... 56
Saratoga Division, Del. & Hud. C. Co's Lines	to Baldwin ... 3
Lake George Steamer	to Caldwell ... 36
Stage	to Glen's Falls ... 9
Saratoga Division, Del. & Hud. C. Co's Lines	to Saratoga ... 23
Saratoga Division, Del. & Hud. C. Co's Lines	to Albany ... 38
Day Line Hudson River Steamers	to New York ... 142

Rate, $43.25

RAILROAD READINGS.

EXCURSION K. X. 189.
New York to Quebec and return.

	MILES
New York, Lake Erie and Western Railroad (via Avon Springs or Portage)	
New York Central and Hudson River R. R.	
Steamer	
Grand Trunk Railway or Royal Mail Line Steamers	
Grand Trunk Railway or Royal Mail Line Steamers	
Grand Trunk Railway	
Passumpsic Railroad	
Montpelier and Wells River R. R.	
Central Vermont R. R.	
Lake Champlain Steamers	
Saratoga Division, Del. & Hud. C. Co's Lines	
Lake George Steamer	
Stage	
Saratoga Division, Del. & Hud. C. Co's Lines	
Saratoga Division, Del. & Hud. C. Co's Lines	
People's (Night) Line Hudson River Steamers	
to Niagara Falls	443
to Lewiston	7
to Toronto	36
to Montreal	333
to Quebec	172
to Sherbrooke	
to Wells River	104
to Montpelier	38
to Burlington	41
to Ft. Ticonderoga	36
to Baldwin	5
to Caldwell	36
to Glen's Falls	9
to Saratoga	23
to Albany	38
to New York	142

Rate, $12.75

Cayuga Lake

HOW TO TAKE OUT THE SCENT.

SITTING on the piazza of the Cataract House, a few Summers ago, was a young, foppish looking gentleman, his garments very highly scented with a mingled odor of musk and cologne. A solemn-faced old man, after passing the dandy several times with a look of aversion which drew general notice, suddenly stopped and in a confidential tone, said:

"Stranger, I know what'll take that scent out of your clothes; you——"

"What do you mean, sir?" said the exquisite, fired with indignation, starting from his chair.

"Oh, get mad now—swear, pitch around and fight, because a man wants to do you a kindness!" coolly replied the stranger. "But I'll tell you I *do know* what'll take out that smell—phew! you must bury your clothes; bury 'em a day or two. Uncle Josh got afoul of a skunk, and he——"

At that instant there went up from the crowd a simultaneous roar of merriment, and the dandy very sensibly "cleared the coop," and rushed up stairs.

AN OLD deacon said to a profane young man, who sat near him in the cars: "You are on the straight road to perdition." The young man drew his ticket from his pocket, and after carefully scrutinizing it, said, "Just my infernal luck. I bought a ticket *for Brunswick.*"

A TALE OF HORROR.

"Old man, old man, for whom digg'st thou
　　this grave?"
　I ask'd as I walk'd along;
For I saw in the heart of London streets
　A dark and a busy throng.

'Twas a strange, wild deed! but a wilder wish
　Of the parted soul, to lie
'Midst the troubled numbers of living men,
　Who would pass him idly by!

So I said, "Old man, for whom digg'st thou
　　this grave
　In the heart of London town?"
And the deep-toned voice of the digger replied
　"We're a laying a gas-pipe down!"

DRIFTING.

IN our picture on the opposite page we
have a delightful summer experience
of floating on gentle waters with fair companions. If life is ever enjoyable, it must
be when friends are together in a boat, gliding under spreading branches, flecked with radiant spots of sunlight, or floating over placid open waters, bathed in the rich glow of the balmy air. A poet writes:

　"All in the gay and golden weather,
　　Two fair maids and an idle man,
　Sailed in a birchen boat together,
　　And sailed the way the river ran.
　The sun was low, not set, and the west
　　Was colored like a robin's breast.
　And they were happy and well content
　　Sailing the way the river went."

Many of us could be content to "sail the way the river went"—to float along through rocky glens, by grassy banks, under shadowy arcades, between sunny meadows, listening to the ripple of the current, and dreaming of a life full of sweetness, like the stream we float upon.

"My Brudders," said a waggish colored man to a crowd, "in all infliction, in all ob yer troubles, dar is one place you can always find sympathy?" "Whar! whar!" shouted several. "In de dictionary," he replied, rolling his eyes skyward.

DRIFTING.

"And they were bound, and he filled a lamp, filled it full to the very brim."

WHITE MOUNTAINS.

EXCURSION K. X. 186.

New York to White Mountains and return.

		MILES.
New York, Lake Erie and Western Railroad (*via* Avon Springs or Portage)	to Niagara Falls	443
New York Central and Hudson River R. R.	to Lewiston	7
Steamer	to Toronto	36
Grand Trunk Railway or Royal Mail Line Steamers	to Montreal	333
Grand Trunk Railway or Royal Mail Line Steamers	to Quebec	172
Grand Trunk Railway	to Gorham	226
Stage	to Glen House	8
Stage	to Tip-Top House	9
Mount Washington Railway	to Base Mt. Wash'n	3
Boston, Concord and Montreal Railroad	to Fabyan House	6
Portland and Ogdensburg R. R.	to Crawford House	5
Portland and Ogdensburg R. R.	to Fabyan House	5
Boston, Concord and Montreal R. R.	to Bethlehem	9
Profile and Franconia Notch R. R.	to Profile House	14
Profile and Franconia Notch R. R.	to Bethlehem	14
Boston, Concord and Montreal R. R.	to Wells River	30
Montpelier and Wells River R. R.	to Montpelier	38
Central Vermont R. R.	to Burlington	41
Lake Champlain Steamers	to Ft. Ticonderoga	56
Saratoga Div., Del. & Hud. C. Co's Lines	to Baldwin	5
Lake George Steamer	to Caldwell	36
Stage	to Glen's Falls	9
Saratoga Div., Del. & Hud. C. Co's Lines	to Saratoga	23
Saratoga Div., Del. & Hud. C. Co's Lines	to Albany	38
Day Line Hudson River Steamers	to New York	142

Rate, - - - $60.25

EXCURSION K. X. 187.

New York to White Mountains and return.

		MILES.
New York, Lake Erie and Western Railroad (*via* Avon Springs or Portage)	to Niagara Falls	443
New York Central and Hudson River R. R.	to Lewiston	7
Steamer	to Toronto	36
Grand Trunk Railway or Royal Mail Line Steamers	to Montreal	333
Grand Trunk Railway or Royal Mail Line Steamers	to Quebec	172
Grand Trunk Railway	to Gorham	226
Stage	to Glen House	8
Stage	to Tip-Top House	9
Mount Washington Railway	to Base Mt. Wash'n	3
Boston, Concord and Montreal R. R.	to Fabyan House	6
Portland and Ogdensburg R. R.	to Crawford House	5
Portland and Ogdensburg R. R.	to Fabyan House	5
Boston, Concord and Montreal R. R.	to Bethlehem	9
Profile and Franconia Notch R. R.	to Profile House	14
Profile and Franconia Notch R. R.	to Bethlehem	14
Boston, Concord and Montreal R. R.	to Wells River	30
Montpelier and Wells River R. R.	to Montpelier	38
Central Vermont R. R.	to Burlington	41
Lake Champlain Steamer	to Ft. Ticonderoga	56
Saratoga Division, Del. & Hud. C. Co's Lines	to Baldwin	5
Lake George Steamer	to Caldwell	36
Stage	to Glen's Falls	9
Saratoga Division, Del. & Hud. C. Co's Lines	to Saratoga	23
Saratoga Division, Del. & Hud. C. Co's Lines	to Albany	38
People's (Night) Line Hudson River Steamers	to New York	142

Rate, - - - $59.75

SUMMER AGAIN.

The softening snow, the ice-bound dripping eaves,
The swelling buds that promise future leaves;
The merry murmur of the road-side stream,
The sunsets fair and gorgeous as a dream—
    All tell of spring.
Another lovely June is near at hand;
Another summer hovers o'er the land;
Soon bright July and sultry August days
Will warm the earth, and hang the hills with haze,
    And pleasure bring.

POLITICAL QUALIFICATIONS.

ABOUT a dozen years ago Governor Y—— and Judge W—— were candidates for Congress in one of the wildest of the Arkansas districts. They were both far-sighted, shrewd politicians—the Judge the better lawyer and debater, the Governor by far the more winning in his manner, as the sequel will fully establish. One hot day in July, while they were travelling together on the canvass, they came upon a party of twenty men or more assembled on the roadside for the purpose of having a shooting-match. Thinking it a good time and place for presenting their respective claims, the Governor proposed stopping. They halted, and the Governor soon made himself at home. He bought a number of chances in the "match," and, being a good marksman, succeeded well, winning quite a quantity of beef, which constituted the prize. The Judge had conscientious scruples as to shooting-matches, and did not participate, but stood by conversing with the more sober of the crowd, while his friend, the Governor, was in high glee with his companions over their beef. When the beef was given out to the successful shooters our Governor ordered his to be divided among some poor widows, who he ascertained lived in the vicinity, and then asked the b'hoys if they were not "dry." Of course they were, and the Governor generously ordered a plentiful supply of the "oh be joyful!" Here again the Judge had scruples, and did not participate; but, had it been otherwise, it would have availed nothing. The Governor was decidedly *the* man at the shooting match, while the Judge felt himself emphatically in the vocative. Leaving their friends, they proceeded on their way some twelve or fifteen miles, and halted at a camp-ground where the annual camp-meeting was being held. They separated in the crowd, each electioneering with all his might, with old and young, friends and strangers—making hay while the sun shone—for there was indeed a fine opening. Toward night the Judge began to look around for his distinguished opponent, but could find him nowhere. He waited patiently till evening services began, and concluded he would go to the large shed where the people had assembled for meeting, thinking perhaps he might meet his friend. On going out, what was his astonishment to find the gallant Governor, the hero of the shooting-match, in front of the altar, surrounded by ministers and class leaders, with a hymn-book in his hand, head thrown back, singing, as loud as lungs would permit.

How firm a foundation, ye saints of the Lord.

"From that moment," said the Judge, "I gave up all hopes. I tell you, a man that's good for a camp-meeting and a shooting match can't be beat for Congress; it can't be done, sir!"

And so it proved.

BILLINGS INSURES HIS LIFE.

I KUM to the conclusion lately that life was so onsartin that the only way for me to stand a fare chance with other folks was to get my life insured, and so I kalled on the agent of the Garden Angel Life Insurance Co., and answered the following questions which were put tu me, over the top of a pair of specs, by a sleek old fellow, with a round gray head on him as any man ever owned: Are yu mail or femail? if so, state how long yu have been so. Had yu a father or mother? if so, which? Are yu subject tu fits? and if so, du yu have mere than one at a time? What is your precise fiting wate? Did yu ever have any ancestors? and if so, how much? Du yu have any nightmare? Are yu married or single, or are yu a bachelor? Have yu ever committed suicide? and if so, how did it affect yu? After answering the above questions like a man in a confirmative, the slick little old fellow with gold specks on sed I was insured fur life, and probably would remain so fur some years. I thanked him, and smiled one ov my most pensive smiles.

A PERSON visiting the London museum, was shown the skull of Oliver Cromwell. "It is extremely small," said the visitor. "Oh," said the guide, "it was his skull when he was a *little boy*."

White Mountains.

EXCURSION K. X. 190.
New York to White Mountains and return.

	MILES.
New York, Lake Erie and Western Railroad (via Avon Springs or Portage)...to Niagara Falls	443
New York Central and Hudson River R. R....to Lewiston	7
Steamer....to Toronto	36
Grand Trunk Railway or Royal Mail Line Steamers....to Montreal	333
Grand Trunk Railway or Royal Mail Line Steamers....to Quebec	172
Grand Trunk Railway....to Sherbrooke	121
Passumpsic Railroad....to Wells River	105
Boston, Concord and Montreal R. R....to Bethlehem	39
Profile and Franconia Notch R. R....to Profile House	14
Profile and Franconia Notch R. R....to Bethlehem	14
Boston, Concord and Montreal R. R....to Fabyan House	9
Portland and Ogdensburg R. R....to Crawford House	5
Portland and Ogdensburg R. R....to Fabyan House	5
Boston, Concord and Montreal R. R....to Wells River	141
Passumpsic R. R....to White Riv. Junc.	40
Central Vermont R. R....to South Vernon	74
Connecticut River R. R....to Springfield	50
New York, New Haven and Hartford R. R....to New York	136

Rate, - - - - $42.50

EXCURSION K. X. 191.
New York to White Mountains and return.

	MILES.
New York, Lake Erie and Western Railroad (via Avon Springs or Portage)...to Niagara Falls	443
New York Central and Hudson River R. R....to Lewiston	7
Steamer....to Toronto	36
Grand Trunk Railway or Royal Mail Line Steamers....to Montreal	333
Grand Trunk Railway....to Gorham	206
Stage....to Glen House	8
Stage....to Tip Top House	9
Mount Washington Railway....to Base Mt. Wash'n.	3
Boston, Concord and Montreal R. R....to Fabyan House	6
Boston, Concord and Montreal R. R....to Bethlehem	9
Profile and Franconia Notch R. R....to Profile House	14
Profile and Franconia Notch R. R....to Bethlehem	14
Boston, Concord and Montreal R. R....to Concord	123
Concord R. R....to Nashua	35
Boston and Lowell R. R....to Boston	40
Sound Steamers (via Fall River or Newport)....to New York	230

Rate - - - - $51.50

EXCURSION K. X. 192.
New York to White Mountains and return.

	MILES.
New York, Lake Erie and Western Railroad (via Avon Springs or Portage)...to Niagara Falls	443
New York Central and Hudson River R. R....to Lewiston	7
Steamer....to Toronto	36
Grand Trunk Railway or Royal Mail Line Steamers....to Montreal	333
Grand Trunk Railway....to Groveton Junc.	175
Boston, Concord and Montreal R. R....to Fabyan House	40
Boston, Concord and Montreal R. R....to Base Mt. Wahs'n.	6
Mount Washington Railway....to Summit	3
Stage....to Glen House	9
Stage....to North Conway	16
Eastern Railroad....to Boston	138
Sound Steamers (via Fall River or Newport)....to New York	230

Rate, - - - - $45.75

RAILROAD READINGS. 55

CORNERING THE BOYS.

ONLY a few days before they moved the capital, a worthy lady of Peoria one morning detected her two sons laughing immoderately. Suspecting she was the cause of their disrespectful mirth, the good woman involuntarily loosened her slipper and called up the young culprits.

"Thomas, what made you laugh?"

"Nobody made me laugh; I laughed on purpose."

"None of your impudence, sir. John, why were you laughing at the door just now?"

John (eagerly)—"Wasn't laughing at the door, I was laughing at Tom."

Tom—"And I was laughing at John."

The matron assumed a dignified attitude. "Now, my boys, what were you both laughing at?"

Boys (in a triumphant shout)— "We were both laughing at once!"

The good lady summoned all her energies for a final effort, and resolved to corner the boys by a settling question.

"Now, then, I want you to tell me, Tom, what made John laugh, and you laugh?"

Tom—"John didn't laugh a new laugh; it was the same old laugh!"

Neither of the boys got whipped, the slipper slid back to its accustomed place, and to this day nobody knows what those boys were laughing at.

AN ILLUSTRATION TURNED.

"I am like Balaam," said a dandy, on meeting a pretty girl in a narrow passage, "stopped by an angel!"

"And I am like an angel," said she, "stopped by an ass!"

A GENTLEMAN recently wrote to certain railroad officials "for a chance to run on the road." He was told he could do so as much as he liked if he would only keep out of the way of trains.

CONTINENTAL HOTEL,

PHILADELPHIA.

J. E. KINGSLEY & CO.,
Proprietors.

ALBEMARLE HOTEL,
EUROPEAN PLAN,
Broadway, Fifth Ave. & 24th St., Madison Square,
NEW YORK.

The attention of the traveling public is especially directed to this Hotel, which is located in the most beautiful portion of the city, and is thoroughly first-class in every respect.

L. H. JANVRIN & CO., Proprietors.

GRAND CENTRAL HOTEL.

COLUMBIA, S. C.

JOHN T. WILLEY, Proprietor.

TERMS FROM $2 TO $3 PER DAY, ACCORDING TO LOCATION OF ROOM.

THE ERIE CANAL.

HERE we stop to view an old familiar sight, two boats passing a canal lock. Our illustration presents a scene at once charming and romantic. Tourists frequently indulge in short trips on the "raging canal." A few days passed aboard one of these boats will afford lots of fun, and make many a new acquaintance. The route traversed by this canal is located along the richest and most beautiful portions of the Empire State, and the traveler never is sea sick, is seldom out of sight of land, and in case of great storms he can jump ashore and put up at any landing for the night. From the tow path and the canal boat have come some of the best men the country has delighted to honor, and statesmen, men great in the field and in the council; and who knows but what the little fellow in our picture may some day hold the helm of the ship of state.

White Mountains.

EXCURSION K. X. 193.
New York to White Mountains and return.

	MILES.
New York, Lake Erie and Western Railroad (via Avon Springs or Portage) ......to Niagara Falls	443
New York Central and Hudson River R. R. ......to Lewiston	7
Steamer ......to Toronto	36
Grand Trunk Railway or Royal Mail Line Steamers ......to Montreal	333
Grand Trunk Railway ......to Rouse's Point	50
Champlain Division, D. & Hud C. Co's Lines ......to Plattsburgh	23
Lake Champlain Steamers ......to Burlington	25
Central Vermont R. R. ......to Montpelier	41
Montpelier Wells River R. R. ......to Wells River	38
Boston, Concord and Montreal R. R. ......to Bethlehem	30
Profile and Franconia Notch R. R. ......to Profile House	14
Profile and Franconia Notch R. R. ......to Bethlehem	14
Boston, Concord and Montreal R. R. ......to Fabyan House	9
Portland and Ogdensburg R. R. ......to Crawford House	5
Portland and Ogdensburg R. R. ......to Fabyan House	5
Boston, Concord and Montreal R. R. ......to Base Mt. Wash'n	6
Mt. Washington Railway ......to Summit	3
Stage ......to Glen House	9
Stage ......to Glen Station	14
Portland and Ogdensburg R. R. ......to Portland	66
Boston and Maine R. R. or Eastern R. R. ......to Bost'n via B. & M. / Eastern	115 / 108
Sound Steamers (via Fall River or Newport) ......to New York	230

Rate, $31.75

EXCURSION K. X. 194.
New York to White Mountains and return.

	MILES.
New York, Lake Erie and Western Railroad (via Avon Springs or Portage) ......to Niagara Falls	443
New York Central and Hudson River R. R. ......to Lewiston	7
Steamer ......to Toronto	36
Grand Trunk Railway or Royal Mail Line Steamers ......to Montreal	333
Grand Trunk Railway or Royal Mail Line Steamers ......to Quebec	172
Grand Trunk Railway ......to Sherbrooke	121
Passumpsic Railroad ......to Wells River	105
Boston, Concord and Montreal R. R. ......to Bethlehem	30
Profile and Franconia Notch R. R. ......to Profile House	14
Profile and Franconia Notch R. R. ......to Bethlehem	14
Boston, Concord and Montreal R. R. ......to Fabyan House	9
Portland and Ogdensburg R. R. ......to Crawford House	5
Portland and Ogdensburg R. R. ......to Fabyan House	5
Boston, Concord and Montreal R. R. ......to Concord	131
Concord R. R. ......to Nashua	35
Boston and Lowell R. R. ......to Boston	40
Sound Steamers (via Fall River or Newport) ......to New York	230

Rate, $45.75

EXCURSION K. X. 195.
New York to White Mountains and return.

	MILES.
New York, Lake Erie and Western Railroad (via Avon Springs or Portage) ......to Niagara Falls	443
New York Central and Hudson River R. R. ......to Lewiston	71
Steamer ......to Toronto	36
Grand Trunk Railway or Royal Mail Line Steamers ......to Montreal	333
Grand Trunk Railway or Royal Mail Line Steamers ......to Quebec	172
Grand Trunk Railway ......to Gorham	226
Stage ......to Glen House	8
Stage ......to Tip-Top House	9
Stage ......to Glen House	9
Stage ......to Glen Station	14
Portland and Ogdensburg R. R. ......to Portland	66
Boston and Maine R. R. or Eastern R. R. ......to Bost'n via B. & M. / East'n	115 / 108
Sound Steamers (via Fall River or Newport) ......to New York	230

Rate, $46.75

LOVE OF NATURE.

Where rose the mountains, there to him were
friends;
Where roll'd the ocean, thereon was his home;
Where a blue sky, and glowing clime extends,
He had the passion and the power to roam.
The desert, forest, cavern, breakers' foam
Were unto him companionship; they spake
A mutual language, clearer than the tone
Of his land's tongue, which he would oft forsake
For Nature's pages, gloss'd by sunbeams on the lake.
Like the Chaldean, he could watch the stars,
Till he had peopled them with beings bright
As their own beams; and earth, and earth-born jars,
And human frailties, were forgotten quite.

THE TRAMP.

A POOR, dejected looking tramp, came limping wearily along till he got a little above Division Street, when he had to pass a knot of young men, and one of them a smart looking young chap, in a very gamey costume, and carrying a broad pair of shoulders and a bullet head, surmounted with a silver-gray plug hat, hung on his right ear, sang out.

"Oh, shoot the hat!"

The poor tramp only looked more dejected than ever, if possible, and shook his head meekly and sorrowfully, and limped on. But the young sport shouted after him:

"Come back, young fellow, and see how you'll trade hats!"

The outcast paused and half turned, and said in mournful tones:

"Don't make game of an onfortnit man, young gents. I'm poor and I'm sick, but I've the feel ins of a man, an' I kin feel it when I'm made game of. If you could give me a job of work, now—"

A chorus of laughter greeted this suggestion, and the smartest young man repeated his challenge to trade hats, and finally induced the mendicant to limp back.

"Take off your hat," said the young man of Burlington, "and let's see whose make it is. If it isn't Stetson's I wont trade."

"Oh, that's Stetson's," chorused the crowd. "He wouldn't wear anything but a first-class hat."

But the tramp replied, trying to limp away from the circle that was closing around him.

"Indeed, young gents, don't be hard on a onfortnit man. I don't believe I could git that hat off'n my head; I don't indeed. I hain't had it off fur mor'n two months, indeed I haint. I don't believe I kin git it off at all. Please let me go on."

But the unfeeling young men crowded around him more closely and insisted that the hat should come off, and the smartest young man in the company said he'd pull it off for him.

"Indeed, young gent," replied the tramp, apologetically, "I don't believe you could get it off. It's been on so long I don't believe you kin git it off; I don't really."

The young man advanced and made a motion to jerk off the hat, but the tramp limped back and threw up his hands with a clumsy frightened gesture.

"Come young gents," he whined, "don't play games on a poor fellow as is lookin' for the county hospital. I tell ye, young gents, I'm a sick man, I am. I'm on the tramp when I ought to be in bed. I can't hardly stand, and I haint got the strength to be fooled with. Be easy on a poor——"

But the sporting young man cut him off with "Oh, give us a rest and take off that hat." And then he made a pass at the poor sick man's hat, but his hand met the poor, sick tramp's elbow instead. And then the poor man lifted one of his hands about as high as a derrick, and the next instant the silver-gray plug hat was crowded so far down on the young man's shoulders that the points of the dog's eared collar were sticking up through the crown of it. And then the poor sick man tried his other hand, and part of the crowd started off to help pick the young man out of a show window where he was standing on his head, while the rest of the congregation was trying their level best to get out of the way of the poor sick tramp, who was feeling about him in a vague, restless sort of way that made the street lamps rattle every time he found anybody. Long before any one could interfere the convention had adjourned *sine die*, and the poor tramp, limping on his way, the very personification of wretchedness, sighed as he remarked apologetically to the spectators:

"I tell you, gents, I'm a sick man, I'm too sick to feel like foolin'; I'm jest so sick that when I go gropin' around for somethin' to lean up agin I can't tell a man from a hitchin' post; I can't actually, and when I rub agin anybody, nobody hadn't ought to feel hard at me. I'm sick, that's what I am."

White Mountains.

EXCURSION K. X. 197.
New York to White Mountains and return.

		MILES.
New York, Lake Erie and Western Railroad (via Avon Springs or Portage)	to Niagara Falls	443
New York Central and Hudson River R. R.	to Lewiston	7
Steamer	to Toronto	36
Grand Trunk Railway or Royal Mail Line Steamers	to Montreal	333
Grand Trunk Railway	to Sherbrooke	101
Passumpsic Railroad	to Wells River	105
Boston, Concord and Montreal R. R.	to Bethlehem	30
Profile and Franconia Notch R. R.	to Profile House	14
Profile and Franconia Notch R. R.	to Bethlehem	14
Boston, Concord and Montreal R. R.	to Fabyan House	9
Portland and Ogdensburg R. R.	to Crawford House	5
Portland and Ogdensburg R. R.	to North Conway	2
Eastern Railroad	to Boston	138
Sound Steamers (via Fall River or Newport)	to New York	230

Rate, - - - $41.50

EXCURSION K. X. 198.
New York to White Mountains and return.

		MILES.
New York, Lake Erie and Western Railroad (via Avon Springs or Portage)	to Niagara Falls	443
New York Central and Hudson River Railroad	to Lewiston	7
Steamer	to Toronto	36
Grand Trunk Railway or Royal Mail Line Steamers	to Montreal	333
Grand Trunk Railway or Royal Mail Line Steamers	to Quebec	172
Grand Trunk Railway	to Gorham	236
Stage	to Glen House	8
Stage	to North Conway	16
Eastern Railroad	to Boston	128
Sound Steamers (via Fall River or Newport)	to New York	230

Rate, - - - $41.50

EXCURSION K. X. 199.
New York to White Mountains and return.

		MILES.
New York, Lake Erie and Western Railroad (via Avon Springs or Portage)	to Niagara Falls	443
New York Central and Hudson River R. R.	to Lewiston	7
Steamer	to Toronto	36
Grand Trunk Railway or Royal Mail Line Steamers	to Montreal	333
Grand Trunk Railway	to Sherbrooke	101
Passumpsic Railroad	to Wells River	105
Boston, Concord and Montreal R. R.	to Bethlehem	30
Profile and Franconia Notch R. R.	to Profile House	14
Profile and Franconia Notch R. R.	to Bethlehem	14
Boston, Concord and Montreal R. R.	to Fabyan House	9
Boston, Concord and Montreal R. R.	to Base Mt. Wash'n.	6
Mt. Washington Railway	to Summit	3
Mt. Washington Railway	to Base Mt. Wash'n.	3
Boston, Concord and Montreal R. R.	to Fabyan House	6
Portland and Ogdensburg R. R.	to Crawford House	5
Portland and Ogdensburg R. R.	to North Conway	27
Eastern Railroad	to Wolfboro	52
Steamer on Lake Winnipiseogee	to Wier's	20
Boston, Concord and Montreal R. R.	to Concord	34
Concord R. R.	to Nashua	35
Boston and Lowell R. R.	to Boston	40
Sound Steamers (via Fall River or Newport)	to New York	230

Rate, - - - $52.50

LABOR, WEALTH, AND PRIDE.

Said Wealth to Pride, one pleasant morn,
  While moving onward on the train,
"I think if you and I were gone,
  The world would strive to move in vain."

"Your words, Sir Wealth, are apt and just,"
  Said Pride; "if we should cease to be,
The world would soon consume with rust,
  Since it is moved by you and me."

Now Labor heard these boastings vain,
  And laying work and care aside,
Said he, "We'll see who moves this train;"
  So down he sat by Wealth and Pride.

But Pride put up her dainty nose,
  And cousin Wealth looked somewhat black,
And now a greater trouble rose—
  The train stood still upon the track.

"Back to your work," cried Wealth and Pride,
  Perceiving, soon, their awkward case:
Wealth twitched his mouth from side to side,
  And Pride grew paler in the face.

But not a word stout Labor said;
  He sat like one in calm repose,
Until Wealth like a suitor plead,
  And Pride let down her haughty nose.

And then, with half-sarcastic mien,
  He calmly rose, and took his place:
The ponderous wheels revolved again—
  The train resumed its wonted place.

Now let us honor Labor more,
  And bow less low to Wealth and Pride;
For Life's the track we're passing o'er—
  The World's the train on which we ride.

"WA'AL, NOW!"

A WELL-KNOWN citizen of Hartford, Connecticut, a few days ago, had taken his seat in the afternoon train for Providence, when a small, weazened-faced, elderly man, having the appearance of a well-to-do farmer, came into the car, looking for a seat. The gentleman good-naturedly made room for him by his side, and the old man looked over him from head to foot.

"Going to Providence?" he said, at length.

"No, sir," the stranger answered, politely; "I stop at Andover."

"I want to know! I belong out that way myself. Expect to stay long?"

"Only over night, sir."

A short pause.

"Did you cal'late to put up at the tavern?"

"No, sir; I expect to stop with Mr. Skinner."

"What, Job Skinner's? Deacon Job lives in a little brown house on the old 'pike? Or, mebbe, it's his brother's? Was it Tim Skinner's —Squire Tim's—where you was goin'?"

"Yes, it was Squire Tim's," said the gentleman, smiling.

"Dew tell if you are goin' there to stop over night. Any connection of his'n?"

"No, sir."

"Well, now, that's curus! The old man ain't got into any trouble, nor nothin', has he?" lowering his voice; "ain't goin' to serve a writ onto him, be ye?"

"Oh, no, nothing of the kind."

"Glad on't. No harm in askin', I s'pose. I reckon *Miss* Skinner's some connection of yourn?"

"No," said the gentleman. Then, seeing the amused expression on the faces of two or three acquaintances in the neighboring seats, he added in a confidential tone: "I am going to see Squire Skinner's daughter."

"Law sakes!" said the old man, his face quivering with curiosity. "*That's* it, is it. I want to know? Goin' to see Mirandy Skinner, be ye? Well, Mirandy's a nice gal kinder humbly, and long favored, but smart to work, they say, and I guess you're about the right age for her too. Kep' company together long?"

"I never saw her in my life, sir."

"How you talk. Somebody's gin her a recommend, I s'pose, and you're gin' clear out there to take a squint at her. Wa'al, I must say there's as likely gals in Andover as Mirandy Skinner. *I've* got a family of grown-up darters myself. Never was married afore, was ye? Don't see no weed on yur hat."

"I have been married about fifteen years, sir I have a wife and five children." And then, as the long restrained mirth of the listeners of this dialogue burst forth at the old man's open mouthed astonishment, he hastened to explain: "I am a doctor, my good friend, and Squire Skinner called at my office this morning, to request my professional services for his sick daughter."

"Wa'al, now!" And the old man here waddled off into the next car.

"YES," said a lawyer who was defending a murderer, "the prisoner at the bar will prove an alibi. Gentlemen, we shall prove that the murdered man wasn't there!"

WOOD ENGRAVING

IN ALL ITS BRANCHES.

ONE THOUSAND ELECTROTYPES FOR SALE.

ADDRESS

SUNSHINE PUBLISHING COMPANY,

306 and 308 Chestnut Street,

PHILADELPHIA.

OVER WATKINS GLEN.

White Mountains.

EXCURSION K. X. 201.
New York to White Mountains and return.

	MILES.
New York, Lake Erie and Western Railroad (via Avon Springs or Portage)	...to Niagara Falls..... 443
New York Central and Hudson River R. R.	...to Lewiston............ 7
Steamer	...to Toronto............ 36
Grand Trunk Railway or Royal Mail Line Steamers	...to Montreal............ 333
Grand Trunk Railway	...to Rouse's Point...... 50
Champlain Division, Del. & Hud. C. Co's Lines	...to Plattsburgh........ 23
Lake Champlain Steamer	...to Burlington......... 25
Central Vermont R. R.	...to Montpelier......... 41
Montpelier and Wells River R. R.	...to Wells River........ 38
Boston, Concord and Montreal R. R.	...to Fabyan House..... 41
Boston, Concord and Montreal R. R.	...to Base Mt. Wash'n. 6
Mt. Washington Railway	...to Summit............. 3
Mt. Washington Railway	...to Base Mt. Wash'n 3
Boston, Concord and Montreal R. R.	...to Fabyan House..... 6
Portland and Ogdensburg R. R.	...to Crawford House.. 5
Portland and Ogdensburg R. R.	...to North Conway.... 27
Eastern Railroad	...to Boston.............. 138
Sound Steamers (via Fall River or Newport)	...to New York.......... 230

Rate, - $47.75

EXCURSION K. X. 202.
New York to White Mountains and return.

	MILES.
New York, Lake Erie and Western Railroad (via Avon Springs or Portage)	...to Niagara Falls..... 443
New York Central and Hudson River R. R.	...to Lewiston............ 7
Steamer	...to Toronto............ 36
Grand Trunk Railway or Royal Mail Line Steamers	...to Montreal............ 333
Grand Trunk Railway	...to Sherbrooke........ 101
Passumpsic Railroad	...to Wells River........ 105
Boston, Concord and Montreal R. R.	...to Bethlehem......... 30
Profile and Franconia Notch R. R.	...to Profile House...... 14
Profile and Franconia Notch R. R.	...to Bethlehem......... 14
Boston, Concord and Montreal R. R.	...to Fabyan House..... 9
Portland and Ogdensburg R. R.	...to Crawford House.. 5
Portland and Ogdensburg R. R.	...to Portland........... 87
Boston and Maine R. R., or Eastern R. R.	...to Bost'n via B. & M. 115 " East'n 108
Sound Steamers (via Fall River or Newport)	...to New York.......... 230

Rate, - - $41.50

EXCURSION No. 50.
New York to White Mountains and return.

	MILES
Fall River Line Steamers	(to Newport or Fall River) 162
Old Colony R. R.	...to Boston.............. 68
Boston and Maine R. R.	...to Portland........... 115
Portland and Ogdensburg R. R.	...to Glen Station....... 66
Stage	...to Glen House........ 14
Stage	...to Sum. Mt. Wash'n 9
Mount Washington Railway	...to Base Mt. Wash'n, 3
Boston, Concord and Montreal Railroad	...to Fabyan House..... 6
Portland and Ogdensburg R. R.	...to Crawford House.. 5
Portland and Ogdensburg R. R.	...to Fabyan House.... 5
Boston, Concord and Montreal R. R.	...to Bethlehem......... 9
Profile and Franconia Notch R. R.	...to Profile House..... 14
Profile and Franconia Notch R. R.	...to Bethlehem......... 14
Boston, Concord and Montreal R. R.	...to Wells River........ 50
Montpelier and Wells River R. R.	...to Montpelier......... 38
Central Vermont R. R.	...to Burlington......... 41
Lake Champlain Steamers	...to Ft. Ticonderoga . 56
Saratoga Div., Del. & Hud. C. Co's Lines	...to Baldwin............ 5
Lake George Steamer	...to Caldwell............ 36
Stage	...to Glen's Falls........ 9
Saratoga Div., Del. & Hud. C. Co's Lines	...to Saratoga............ 23
Saratoga Div., Del. & Hud. C. Co's Lines	...to Albany............. 38
New York Central and Hudson River R. R.	...to Niagara Falls...... 306
New York, Lake Erie and Western Railroad (via Avon Springs or Portage)	to New York.......... 443

Rate, - - - $50.75

POET-TREE.

Oak, Caroline! fir yew 1 pine;
O, willow, will you not be mine?
Thy hazel eyes, thy tulips red,
Thy ways, all larch, have turned my head;
All linden shadows by the gate,
I cypress on my heart and wait;
Then gum! beech-cherished Caroline:
We'll fly for elms of bliss divine.

O, spruce young man! I cedar plan
Catalpa's money, if you can;
You sumach ash, but not my heart:
You're evergreen, so now depart;
You'd like to poplar—that I see
Birch you walnut propose to me—
Here's pa! you'll see hemlock the gate:
He maple-litely say "'tis late."

Locust that lovyer, while he flew
For elms before that parent's shoe;
He little thought a dogwood bite
And make him balsam much that night,
Hawthorney path he traveled o'er,
And he was sick and sycamore.

NEVER SAW ONE OF THEM.

AT the Sutter house, Sacramento, a New Yorker newly arrived, was lamenting his condition and his folly of leaving an abundance at home, and especially two beautiful daughters who were just budding into womanhood; when he asked the other if he had a family. "Yes, sir: I have a wife and six children in New York, and I never saw one of them." After this reply the couple sat a few moments in silence, and then the interrogator again commenced. "Were you ever blind, sir?" "No, sir." "Did you marry a widow, sir?" "No, Sir." Another lapse of silence. "Did I understand you to say, sir, that you had a wife and six children living in New York, and had never seen one of them?" "Yes, sir: I so stated it." Another and a longer pause of silence. Then the interrogator again inquired. "How can it be, sir, that you never saw one of them?" "Why," was the response, "*one of them* was born after I left." "Oh! ah!" and a general laugh followed. After that the first New Yorker was especially distinguished as "the man who has six children, and never saw one of them."

WOMAN is a natural traveler. It is a study to see her start off on a trip by herself. She comes down to the depot in an express wagon three hours before train time. She insists on sitting on her trunk, out on the platform, to keep it from being stolen. She picks up her reticule, fan, parasol, lunch basket, small pot with a house plant in it, shawl, paper bag of candy, bouquet (she never travels without one), small tumbler and extra veil, and chases histerically after every switch-engine that goes by, under the impression that it is her train. Her voice trembles as she presents herself at the restaurant and tries to buy a ticket, and she knocks with the handle of her parasol on the door of the old disused tool-house in vain hopes that the baggage man will come out and check her trunk. She asks every body in the depot and on the platform when her train will start, and where it will stand, and, looking straight at the great clock, asks: "What time is it now?" She sees, with terror, the baggage man shy her trunk into a car where two men are smoking, instead of locking it up by itself in a large strong brown car with "Bad order, shops," chalked on the side, which she has long ago determined to be the baggage car as the only safe one in sight. Although the first at the depot, she is the last to get her ticket; and once on the cars, she sits, to the end of her journey, in an agony of apprehension that she has got on the wrong train and will be landed at some strange station, put in a close carriage, drugged, and murdered, and to every last male passenger who walks down the aisle she stands up and presents her ticket, which she invariably carries in her hand. She finally recognizes her waiting friends on the platform, leaves the car in a burst of gratitude, and the train is ten miles away before she remembers that her reticule, fan, parasol, lunch basket, verbena, shawl, candy, tumbler, veil, and bouquet, are on the car seat where she left them, or at the depot in Peoria, for the life of her she can't tell which.

"A MERCIFUL man," tenderly remarked a Ninth Street man one bitter cold January morning, "is merciful to his beast," and he called the dog in out of the snow, gave him his breakfast in a soup plate, and laid a piece of carpet down behind the kitchen stove for him to snooze on. Then the man went down town, and the neighbors watched his wife shovel snow-paths to the woodshed, cistern, stable, and front gate, and then do an hour's work cleaning off the sidewalk.

FULFILLING DIRECTIONS.—A Quaker, in business in Philadelphia, disliking the "Esq." to his name, advised a correspondent to direct his letters to him without any tail, and received a reply superscribed, "Amos Smith, without any tail, Philadelphia!"

White Mountains.

EXCURSION No. 51.
New York to White Mountains and return.

		MILES.
Fall River Line Steamers..	{ to Newport or } { Fall River.... }	162
Old Colony R. R..	....to Boston................	68
Eastern Railroad...	....to North Conway.....	138
Portland and Ogdensburg R. R.........................	....to Crawford House..	27
Portland and Ogdensburg R. R....................	....to Fabyan House.....	5
Boston, Concord and Montreal R. R...	....to Wells River.........	41
Passumpsic Railroad...	....to White Riv. Junc.	40
Central Vermont R. R............................	....to South Vernon......	74
Connecticut River R. R.......................................	....to Springfield..........	50
Boston and Albany R. R................................	....to Albany................	103
Saratoga Division, Del. & Hud. C. Co's Lines...............	....to Saratoga.............	38
Saratoga Division, Del. & Hud. C. Co's Lines.................	....to Schenectady........	21
New York Central and Hudson River R. R...............................	....to Niagara Falls......	289
New York, Lake Erie and Western Railroad (via Avon Springs or Portage).......	....to New York............	443

Rate, - - - - $34.10

EXCURSION No. 52.
New York to White Mountains and return.

		MILES.
Fall River Line Steamers...	{ to Newport or } { Fall River }	162
Old Colony R. R..	....to Boston................	68
Boston and Lowell R. R...	....to Nashua...............	40
Concord R. R...	....to Concord,.............	35
Boston, Concord and Montreal R. R...............	....to Fabyan House.....	134
Boston, Concord and Montreal R. R...................	....to Bethlehem..........	9
Profile and Franconia Notch R. R........	....to Profile House......	14
Profile and Franconia Notch R. R.....	....to Bethlehem..........	14
Boston, Concord and Montreal R. R.....	....to Wells River.........	30
Montpelier Wells River R. R..................	....to Montpelier.........	38
Central Vermont R. R.................................	....to Burlington..........	41
Lake Champlain Steamers...............................	....to Ft. Ticonderoga..	56
Saratoga Division, Del. & Hud. C. Co's Lines........	....to Baldwin..............	5
Lake George Steamer...	....to Caldwell.............	36
Stage...	....to Glen's Falls........	9
Saratoga Div., Del. and Hud. C. Co's Lines...............	....to Saratoga.............	23
Saratoga Div., Del. and Hud. C. Co's Lines.............	....to Albany................	38
New York Central and Hudson River R. R.................................	....to Niagara Falls......	306
New York, Lake Erie and Western Railroad (via Avon Springs or Portage)........	....to New York............	443

Rate, - - - - $38.95

EXCURSION No. 53.
New York to White Mountains and return.

		MILES.
New York, Lake Erie and Western Railroad (via Avon Springs or Portage)................	....to Niagara Falls......	443
New York Central and Hudson River R. R..	....to Schenectady........	289
Saratoga Division, Del. & Hud. C. Co's Lines (via Saratoga)................................	....to Glen's Falls.........	45
Stage..	....to Caldwell..............	9
Lake George Steamer................................	....to Baldwin...............	36
Saratoga Division, Del. & Hud. C. Co's Lines..............	....to Ft. Ticonderoga..	5
Lake Champlain Steamers.............................	....to Burlington..........	56
Central Vermont R. R...	....to Montpelier.........	41
Montpelier and Wells R. R..........................	....to Wells River.........	38
Boston, Concord and Montreal R. R................	....to Fabyan House.....	41
Boston, Concord and Montreal R. R................	....to Base Mt. Wash'n.	6
Mt. Washington Railway.................................	....to Summit...............	3
Mt. Washington Railway.................................	....to Base Mt. Wash'n.	3
Boston, Concord and Montreal R. R................	....to Fabyan House.....	6
Portland and Ogdensburg R. R.....................	....to Crawford House..	5
Portland and Ogdensburg R. R.....................	....to Fabyan House.....	5
Boston, Concord and Montreal R. R................	....to Bethlehem..........	9
Profile and Franconia Notch R. R..............	....to Profile House......	14
Profile and Franconia Notch R. R..............	....to Bethlehem..........	14
Boston, Concord and Montreal R. R................	....to Concord..............	123
Concord R. R..	....to Nashua...............	35
Boston and Lowell R. R.............................	....to Boston................	40
Old Colony R. R..	{ to Fall River or } { Newport........ }	68
Fall River Line Steamers................................	....to New York............	162

Rate, - - - - $44.15

THE GLADNESS OF NATURE.

There are notes of joy from the hang-bird and wren,
  And the gossip of swallows through all the sky;
The ground-squirrel gaily chirps by his den,
  And the wilding-bee hums merrily by.

The clouds are at play in the azure space,
  And their shadows at play on the bright green vale,
And here they stretch to the frolic chase,
  And there they roll on the easy gale.

There's a dance of leaves in that aspen bower;
  There's a titter of winds in that beechen tree;
There's a smile on the fruit, a smile on the flower,
  And a laugh from the brook that runs to the sea.

ATTEMPTED CONUNDRUMS.

A PARTY of gentlemen were wont to amuse themselves at table by relating anecdotes, conundrums, etc. A Mr. A was always greatly delighted at these jokes, but never related any thing himself, and being rallied on the matter he determined that the next time he was called upon he would say something amusing. Accordingly, meeting one of the waiters soon afterward he asked him if he knew any good jokes or conundrums. The waiter told him that he did, and related the following: "It is my father's child, and my mother's child, yet it is not my sister or brother," telling him at the same time that it was himself. The gentleman bore this in mind, and at the next gathering he suddenly burst out with "I've got a conundrum for you." "Propound it then," exclaimed his companions. "It's my father's child, and my mother's child, yet is not my sister or brother," said the gentleman, throwing a triumphant glance across the tables. "Then it must be yourself," said one of the company. "I've got you now," said he; "you are wrong this time; it is the waiter." A shout of laughter interrupted A., who perceiving the mess he had got into acknowledged his error and told the company that he would pay for the wine. That was A's last effort.

THEY were very pretty, and there was apparently five or six years difference in their ages. As the train pulled up at Bussey, the young girl blushed, flattened her nose nervously against the window, and drew back in joyous smiles as a young man came dashing into the car, shook hands tenderly and cordially, insisted on carrying her valise, magazine, little paper bundle, and would probably have carried herself had she permitted him. The passengers smiled as she left the car, and the murmur went rippling through the coach. "They're engaged." The other girl sat looking nervously out of the window, and once or twice gathered her parcels together as though she would leave the car, yet seemed to be expecting some one. At last he came. He bulged in at the door like a house on fire, looked along the seats until his gaze fell on her upturned expectant face, roared, "Come on! I've been waiting for you on the platform for fifteen minutes!" grabbed her basket, and strode out of the car, while she followed with a little valise, a band-box, a paper bag full of lunch, a bird-cage, a glass jar of jelly, and an extra shawl. And a crusty-looking old bachelor, in the farther end of the car, croaked out, in unison with the indignant looks of the passengers, "They're married!"

MANSION HOUSE,
MAUCH CHUNK, PENNA.

JAS. S. WIBIRT, Proprietor.

ROCKINGHAM HOUSE,

FRANK W. HILTON, Proprietor.

PORTSMOUTH, N. H.

The fittings, appointments, and *cuisine*, of the "Rockingham" are *unsurpassed* by those of any Hotel in New England.

THE DEDICATION.

A wit and an illiterate fop
Once met in a bookseller's shop;
The coxcomb cast a sage-like look
On many a gilt and letter'd book,
Took up a volume, threw it down.
Assuming a contemptuous frown.
The wit, with seeming serious air
Bespoke him thus: "Sir, I declare
Here is a book inscribed to you!"
"Impossible!" "'Tis very true.
He snatched it, with "Pray let me see
His name, who so much honors me;"
And read aloud this dedication
"To every numskull in the nation!"

"TECHING THE BOTTOM."

TWO raftsmen were caught in the late big blow on the Mississippi, when so many rafts were swamped and so many steamboats lost their sky riggings. The raft was just emerging from Lake Pepin as the squall came. In an instant it was pitching and writhing, as if suddenly dropped into Charybdis, while the waves broke over it with tremendous uproar. Expecting instant destruction, the raftsmen dropped on their knees and commenced praying with a power equal to the emergency. Happening to open his eyes, he observed his companion, not engaged in prayer, but pushing a pole in the water at the side of the raft. "What's that yer doin', Mike?" said he; "get down on yer knees now, for there isn't a minute between us and purgatory." "Be aisy, Pat," said the other, as he coolly continued to punch with his pole; "what's the use of prayin' when a feller can tech bottom with a pole?" Mike is a pretty specimen of a large class of Christians, who prefer to omit prayer as long as they can "tech bottom."

HELPED. — "I'd like you to help me a little," said a vagrant, poking his head into a country store. "Why don't you help yourself?" asked the proprietor. "Thank you, I will," said the tramp, picking up a bottle of pickles and two loaves of bread, and then vanishing.

SONG OF SONGS.

The leaf tongues of the forest, the flower tips of the sod,
The happy birds that hymn their rapture in the ear of God,
The summer wind that bringeth music over land and sea,
Have each a voice that singeth this sweet song of songs to me.
The world is full of beauty, like other worlds above,
And if we do our duty it might be full of love.

THE ARAB'S ANSWER.

A STORY is told by Lamartine, of an Arab named Naher, who owned a very fleet and beautiful horse. A Bedouin, Daher, tried in vain to buy him; and, determined on his possession, disguised himself as a lame beggar, and crouched by the roadside where he expected Naher to pass. When he saw him approaching, mounted on his beautiful steed, he hailed him in a weak voice, and implored his aid, saying he had been unable for three days to move from that spot, and was faint from hunger and thirst.

"Get on my horse behind me," said the kind-hearted Arab, instantly, "and I will carry you where you want to go."

Daher pretended to try to rise, failing to do so, of course; and Naher, as he expected, dismounted and placed the beggar in the saddle. Instantly the villain put the horse to his utmost speed, looking back to call out, "I am Daher; I have your horse, and I will keep him!"

Naher shouted to him to stop a moment and listen; and Daher, sure of not being overtaken, stopped.

"You have taken my horse," said Naher; "since Heaven has permitted it, I still wish you well, but I conjure you never to tell any one how you obtained him."

"And why?" asked Daher in surprise.

"Because many a one whose heart is pitiful would pass by distress, suspicious of deception. Lest they should be duped as I have been, they would refuse aid really needed, and which would

otherwise be given."

Daher paused, in utter shame.

Presently he turned, rode back to Naher, and restored his horse—and thus began a friendship that lasted for life.

"Pull out, Bill!" shrieked an engineer's son to one of his playmates, a brakeman's boy, who was in immediate danger of getting smashed by his mother, who was coming after him. "Git on the main line and give her steam! Here comes the switch engine!" But before the juvenile could get in motion, she had him by the ear, and he was laid up with a hot box.

THE PICNIC.

WHO has not picnicked in the woods, and enjoyed it vastly, too. Oh, for those days of fun and frolic and freedom to return. Pshaw man, cease your yearnings. Call at any office of the Erie Railway, tell the ticket agent all your wants and with a guide book in your hand he will inform you of the shortest and most pleasant route to vales of indescribable loveliness, where, in company with a few friends, you can have heaven on earth. There is a time for everything, and our advice to all tired city ones is to make this season one of sweet adventure in the woods, where the streamlets are and the birds love to sing.

A TUTOR of one of the Oxford Colleges, who limped in his walk, was some years ago accosted by a well-known politician, who asked him if he was not the chaplain of the college at such a time, naming the year. The doctor replied that he was. The interrogator observed, "I knew you by your limp." "Well," said the doctor, "it seems my limping made a deeper impression than my preaching." "Ah, doctor," was the reply, with ready wit, "it is the highest compliment we can pay a minister, to say that he is known by his walk, rather than by his conversation."

AN ARTIST in New Jersey painted a dog so naturally, that the animal had the hydrophobia during the dog days. He painted a beer bottle with such skill, that the cork flew out just as he was finishing it. After he married, he painted a picture of his first baby, so life like, that it cried, and his wife whipped it before she discovered her mistake

A Picnic in the Woods.

II.

Excursions Starting from New York and Terminating at Other Points.

SARATOGA.

EXCURSION K. X. 18.
New York to Saratoga.

	MILES.
New York, Lake Erie and Western Railroad (via Avon Springs or Portage) ......to Niagara Falls	443
New York Central and Hudson River R. R. ......to Lewiston	7
Steamer ......to Toronto	36
Grand Trunk Railway or Royal Mail Line Steamers ......to Montreal	333
Grand Trunk Railway ......to Rouse's Point	50
Champlain Division, Del. & Hud. C. Co's Lines ......to Plattsburgh	23
Champlain Division, Del. & Hud. C. Co's Lines or Lake Champlain Steamer ......to Ft. Ticonderoga	68
Saratoga Division, Del. & Hud. C. Co's Lines ......to Baldwin	5
Lake George Steamer ......to Caldwell	36
Stage ......to Glen's Falls	9
Saratoga Division, Del. & Hud. C. Co's Lines ......to Saratoga	23

Rate, - - - $31.00

EXCURSION K. X. 28.
New York to Saratoga.

	MILES.
New York, Lake Erie and Western Railroad (via Avon Springs or Portage) ......to Niagara Falls	443
New York Central and Hudson River R. R. ......to Lewiston	7
Steamer ......to Toronto	36
Grand Trunk Railway or Royal Mail Line Steamers ......to Montreal	333
Grand Trunk Railway ......to Rouse's Point	50
Champlain Division, Del. & Hud. C. Co's Lines ......to Plattsburgh	23
Champlain Division, Del. & Hud. C. Co's Lines or Lake Champlain Steamer ......to Ft. Ticonderoga	68
Saratoga Division, Del. & Hud. C. Co's Lines ......to Saratoga	61

Rate, - - - $28.25

MONTREAL.

EXCURSION K. X. 6.
New York to Montreal.

	MILES.
New York, Lake Erie and Western Railroad (via Avon Springs or Portage) ......to Niagara Falls	443
New York Central and Hudson River R. R. ......to Lewiston	7
Steamer ......to Toronto	36
Grand Trunk Railway or Royal Mail Line Steamers ......to Montreal	333

Rate, - - - $20.50

EXCURSION No. 54.
New York to Montreal.

	MILES.
New York, Lake Erie and Western Railroad (via Avon Springs or Portage) ......to Niagara Falls	443
New York Central and Hudson River R. R. ......to Utica	211
Utica and Black River R. R. (via Trenton Falls) ......to Clayton	108
Steamer ......to Alexandria Bay	12
Royal Mail Line Steamers ......to Montreal	165

Rate, - - - $21.00

EXCURSION No. 53.
New York to Montreal.

	MILES.
New York, Lake Erie and Western Railroad (via Avon Springs or Portage) ......to Niagara Falls	443
New York Central and Hudson River R. R. ......to Syracuse	158
Rome, Watertown and Ogdensburg R. R. ......to Cape Vincent	95
Steamer ......to Alexandria Bay	30
Royal Mail Line Steamers ......to Montreal	165

Rate, - - - $21.00

HAPPINESS.

There is a gentler element, and man
May breathe it with a calm unruffled soul,
And drink its living waters till the heart
Is pure. And this is human happiness!
Its secret and its evidence are writ
In the broad book of nature. 'Tis to have
Attentive and believing faculties;
To go abroad rejoicing in the joy
Of beautiful and well created things;
To love the voice of waters, and the sheen
Of silver fountains leaping to the sea;
To thrill with the rich melody of birds
Loving their life of music; to be glad
In the gay sunshine, reverent in the storm;
To see a beauty in the stirring leaf
And find calm thoughts beneath the whispering
tree;

A BATCH OF CONUNDRUMS.

"TALK of conundrums," said Old Hurricane, stretching himself all over Social Hall, and sending out one of those mighty puffs of Havana smoke which has given him his name, "can any of you tell me when a ship may be said to be in love?" "I can tell— I can," snapped out little Turtle. "it's when she wants to be manned." "Just missed it," quoth Old Hurricane. "try again who speaks first?" "I do, secondly," answered Lemon. "it's when she wants a mate." "Not correct," replied Hurricane, "the question is still open." "When she's a ship of great size," sighs modestly propounded Mr. Smoothly. "When she *tenders to a man of war*," said the Colonel, regarding the reflection of his face in his boots. "Everything but correct," responded Hurricane. "When she's struck aback by a heavy swell," suggested Starlight. "Not as yet," said Hurricane. "come, hurry along." "When she *makes much of a fast sailor*," cried Smashpipes. Here there was a great groan. When peace was restored Old Hurricane propelled "again." "You might have said, When she's run down after a smack, or When she's after a consort, or something of that sort, but it wouldn't have been right. The real solution is, when she's attached to *a buoy*."

The Whirling Waters.

NEXT TIME YOU GO WEST
TRY
THE 6 P.M.
NEW TRAIN
ON THE
NEW YORK, LAKE ERIE AND WESTERN RAILWAY.
(FORMERLY ERIE.)

It leaves New York from Chambers Street Depot at **6** P. M.; and from 23rd Street Depot at **5.45** P. M., every day in the week, and is called

FAST ST. LOUIS EXPRESS,

Because it carries you to Cleveland, Toronto, Detroit, Toledo, Indianapolis, St. Louis, and points beyond, *as quickly* as any other train in the United States; and to

BUFFALO *25 Minutes Earlier than any Competing Line.*

This Train is equipped with the famous Westinghouse Air Brakes, under the instantaneous control of the engineer; the Miller Platforms, Couplers and Buffers between the cars, and the finest PULLMAN SLEEPING COACHES in the world, without exception.

No other Railway between New York and the West has these combined appliances, securing Speed, Safety and Comfort in traveling thus offered via ERIE RAILWAY.

JNO. N. ABBOTT,
General Passenger Agent, NEW YORK.

WATKINS GLEN.

Rainbow Falls.

A RAMBLE through Watkins Glen, even at present, is a real and delightful. Excepting Niagara itself, no place will bear comparison with this wild and picturesque gorge. Our illustration represents the famous Rainbow Falls.

Quebec—Portland—Boston.

QUEBEC.
EXCURSION K. X. 7.
New York to Quebec.

	MILES
New York, Lake Erie and Western Railroad (via Avon Springs or Portage)	...to Niagara Falls...... 443
New York Central and Hudson River R. R.	...to Lewiston............ 7
Steamer	...to Toronto............ 36
Grand Trunk Railway or Royal Mail Line Steamers	...to Montreal............ 333
Grand Trunk Railway or Royal Mail Line Steamers	...to Quebec............. 172

Rate, - - - - $23.00

PORTLAND.
EXCURSION K. X. 10.
New York to Portland.

	MILES
New York, Lake Erie and Western Railroad (via Avon Springs or Portage)	...to Niagara Falls...... 443
New York Central and Hudson River R. R.	...to Lewiston............ 7
Steamer	...to Toronto............ 36
Grand Trunk Railway or Royal Mail Line Steamers	...to Montreal............ 333
Grand Trunk Railway or Royal Mail Line Steamers	...to Quebec............. 172
Grand Trunk Railway	...to Portland............ 317

Rate, - - - - $30.00

EXCURSION K. X. 14.
New York to Portland.

	MILES
New York, Lake Erie and Western Railroad (via Avon Springs or Portage)	to Niagara Falls...... 443
New York Central and Hudson River R. R.	to Lewiston............ 7
Steamer	to Toronto............ 36
Grand Trunk Railway or Royal Mail Line Steamers	to Montreal............ 333
Grand Trunk Railway	...to Portland............ 297

Rate, - - - - $27.00

BOSTON.
EXCURSION K. X. 11.
New York to Boston.

	MILES
New York, Lake Erie and Western Railroad (via Avon Springs or Portage)	...to Niagara Falls...... 443
New York Central and Hudson River R. R.	...to Lewiston............ 7
Steamer	...to Toronto............ 36
Grand Trunk Railway or Royal Mail Line Steamers	...to Montreal............ 333
Grand Trunk Railway or Royal Mail Line Steamers	...to Quebec............. 172
Grand Trunk Railway	...to Portland............ 317
Boston and Maine R. R.	...to Boston............. 115

Rate, - - - - $31.50

EXCURSION K. X. 15.
New York to Boston.

	MILES
New York, Lake Erie and Western Railroad (via Avon Springs or Portage)	...to Niagara Falls...... 443
New York Central and Hudson River R. R.	...to Lewiston............ 7
Steamer	...to Toronto............ 36
Grand Trunk Railway or Royal Mail Line Steamers	...to Montreal............ 333
Grand Trunk Railway	...to Portland............ 297
Eastern Railroad	...to Boston............. 106

Rate, - - - - $28.50

EXCURSION K. X. 183.
New York to Boston.

	MILES
New York, Lake Erie and Western Railroad (via Avon Springs or Portage)	...to Niagara Falls...... 443
New York Central and Hudson River R. R.	...to Lewiston............ 7
Steamer	...to Toronto............ 36
Grand Trunk Railway or Royal Mail Line Steamers	...to Montreal............ 333
Grand Trunk Railway	...to Rouse's Point...... 50
Champlain Division, Del. & Hud. C. Co's Lines	...to Plattsburgh........ 23
Lake Champlain Steamer	...to Burlington......... 25
Central Vermont R. R.	...to Montpelier......... 41
Montpelier and Wells River R. R.	...to Wells River........ 38
Boston, Concord and Montreal R. R.	...to Concord............ 93
Concord Railroad	...to Nashua............. 35
Boston, Lowell and Nashua R. R.	...to Boston............. 40

Rate, - - - $33.50

CHEMUNG VALLEY.

NEAR Waverly the Susquehanna River sweeps away to the southward, and the Chemung Valley is entered. This is one of the most picturesque and attractive spots in southern New York; it is simply a panorama of unfolding loveliness. Don't fail to visit it if possible. The view from the bridge is superbly beautiful, and one never to be forgotten.

III.
SIDE TRIP, OR EXTENSION EXCURSIONS.

EXCURSION A.
Elmira to Watkins' Glen and return.

		MILES
Northern Central R. R.	to Watkins' Glen	22
Northern Central R. R.	to Elmira	22

Rate,   90 Cts.

EXCURSION T.
Lackawaxen to Carbondale, and return (Del. and Hud. C. Co's Gravity R. R.)

		MILES
New York, Lake Erie and Western Railroad	to Honesdale	25
Omnibus	to D. and H. C. Co's Depot	1
Del. and Hud. C. Co's Gravity R. R.	to Carbondale	16
Del. and Hud. C. Co's Gravity R. R.	to Honesdale	18
Omnibus	to N. Y., L. E. and W. Depot	1
New York, Lake Erie and Western Railroad	to Lackawaxen	25

Rate, $2.25

EXCURSION W.
Lackawaxen to Dunmore (Scranton) and return (Penna. Coal Co's Gravity R. R.)

		MILES
New York, Lake Erie and Western Railroad	to Hawley	16
Penn. Coal Co's Gravity R. R.	to Dunmore	33
Penn. Coal Co's Gravity R. R.	to Hawley	33
New York, Lake Erie and Western Railroad	to Lackawaxen	16

Rate, $2.15

EXCURSION Y.
Lackawaxen to Scranton and return (Del. and Hud. C. Co's Gravity R. R., and Penna. Coal Co's Gravity R. R.)

		MILES
New York, Lake Erie and Western Railroad	to Honesdale	25
Omnibus	to D. & H. C. Co's Depot	1
Del. and Hud. C. Co's Gravity R. R.	to Carbondale	16
Omnibus	to D. & H. C. Co's Depot	1
Penn. Div., Del. and Hud. C. Co's Lines	to Scranton	15
People's Passenger Railway	to Dunmore	1½
Penna. Coal Co's Gravity R. R.	to Hawley	33
New York, Lake Erie and Western Railroad	to Lackawaxen	16

Rate, $2.80

EXCURSION Z.
Lackawaxen to Scranton and return (Penn. C. Co's Gravity R. R., and Del. and Hud. C. Co's Gravity R. R.)

		MILES
New York, Lake Erie and Western Railroad	to Hawley	16
Penn. Coal Co's Gravity R. R.	to Dunmore	33
People's Passenger Railway	to Scranton	1½
Penn. Div., Del. and Hud. C. Co's Lines	to Carbondale	16
Omnibus	to D. and H. Gravity R. R. Depot	1
Del. and Hud. C. Co's Gravity R. R.	to Honesdale	18
Omnibus	to N. Y., L. E. and W. Depot	1
New York, Lake Erie and Western Railroad	to Lackawaxen	25

Rate, $2.80

*NOTE—Although Excursion Z is the reverse of the preceding one, it covers different ground, as Excursion Y traverses only *one half* of the *round trip loop* of each Gravity R. R., while Excursion Z traverses the remaining half.

I AM COMING.

I am coming! I am coming,
  Sings the robin on the wing;
Soon the gates of spring will open;
  Where you loiter I will sing;
Turn your thoughts to merriest music,
  Send it ringing down the vale,
Where the yellow bird is waiting
  On the old brown meadow-rail!

I am coming! I am coming!
  Sings the summer from afar,
And her voice is like the shining
  Of some silver-mantled star;
In it breathes the breath of flowers,
  In it hides the dawn of day,
In it wake the happy showers
  Of the merry, merry May!

DIAMOND CUT DIAMOND.

ANDY CUMMINS was a "cute down easter"—a real live Yankee, hard to beat. He was once in a country bar-room "down south," where several gentlemen were assembled, when one of them said, "Cummins, if you'll go out and stick your penknife into anything, when you come back I'll tell you what it's sticking in." "Yer can't do no sich thing," responded Cummins. "I'll bet ten dollars on it," answered the Southerner. "Wal, I rather guess I'll take that ere bet. Here, captain," turning to the landlord, "hold stakes, and I'll just make half a saw-horse in less than no time." The parties deposited an X apiece, and C. departed on his mission, but in a short time returned, saying, "Wal, neighbor, what's it sticking in?" "In the handle," replied the Southerner, holding out his hand for the stakes. "Guess not; jist wait a minit," said the Yankee, holding up the handle of his knife minus the blade. "I kalkilate the blade can't be in the handle when it's drive clean up in an old stump aside of yer road out thar." Cummins, of course, won the wager, and the Southerner sloped for parts unknown, amid roars of laughter.

You should bear constantly in mind that nine-tenths of us are, from the very nature and necessities of the world, born to earn our livelihood by the sweat of the brow? What reason have we then to presume that our children are not to do the same? If they be, as now and then one will be, endowed with extraordinary powers of mind, those powers may have an opportunity of developing themselves; and if they never have that opportunity the harm is not very great to us or to them. Nor does it hence follow that the descendants of laborers are always to be laborers. The path upward is steep and long to be sure. Industry, care, skill, excellence in the present parent, lay the foundation of a rise under more favorable circumstances for the children. The children of these take another rise; and by-and-by the descendants of the present laborer become gentlemen. This is the natural progress. It is by attempting to reach the top at a single leap that so much misery is produced in the world; and the propensity to make such attempt has been cherished and encouraged by the strange projects that we have witnessed of late years for making the laborers virtuous and happy by giving them what is called education. The education which I speak of consists in bringing up children to labor with steadiness, with care, and with skill; to show them how to do as many useful things as possible, to teach them how to do them in the best manner; to set them an example of industry, sobriety, cleanliness, and neatness; to make all these habitual to them, so that they shall never be liable to fall into the contrary; to let them always see a good living proceeding from labor, and thus to remove from them the temptation to get at the goods of others by violent or fraudulent means, and to keep far from their minds all the inducements to hypocrisy and deceit.

"COMPLIMENTS EXTRAORDINARY."—"Will you please to insert this obituary notice," wrote a country editor's correspondent. "I make bold to ask it, because I knew the deceased had a great many friends who would be glad to hear of his death.'" This anecdote is equaled by what occurred in connection with an Edinburgh newspaper less than ten years ago. One morning a notice appeared of the death of a clergyman, in which his good qualities were duly narrated, and his weaknesses thinly veiled. The editor, in the course of the day, was startled to find his sanctum invaded by the supposed defunct minister. Of course regret was expressed, and a public contradiction was promised. Next morning an announcement to the following effect appeared:—"We regret to state that the report we published yesterday of the death of Rev. Mr. —— is not true."

HOFFMAN HOUSE.

RESTAURANT AND CAFÉ,
MADISON SQUARE.
NEW YORK.

A favorite family Hotel. Rates as reasonable as any. Rooms $1.00 and upwards.

C. H. READ, Proprietor.

WINDSOR HOTEL,
FIFTH AVENUE, 46th & 47th STREETS, NEW YORK.
HAWK & WETHERBEE, Proprietors.

The Windsor is more magnificent and commodious, and contains more real comforts, than any other Hotel in America. Its location is delightful, being surrounded by the most fashionable residences in New York; it is also near the famous Central Park and within three minutes' walk of the Grand Central Railway Station. The rooms with all the modern improvements are especially adapted for travelers; this Hotel also has elegant apartments, en suite for families, permanent and transient. The light, ventilation, and sanitary qualities are perfect, and are not excelled by any hotel on either continent. Its table is of unexceptionable excellence.

SAMUEL HAWK   GARDNER WETHERBEE

"TAYLOR'S."

St. Denis Hotel and Restaurant.

Broadway, corner 11th Street,
NEW YORK.

Mauch Chunk Switchback—Geneva—Trenton Falls, etc.

EXCURSION E.
Mauch Chunk to Summit Hill and return.

		MILES.
Switch Back R. R. (with Omnibus Transfer)	...to Summit Hill.	9
Switch Back R. R. (with Omnibus Transfer)	...to Mauch Chunk.	9

Rate, - - - $1.25

EXCURSION J.
Mauch Chunk to Summit Hill and return.

		MILES
Switch Back R. R.	...to Summit Hill...	9
Switch Back R. R.	...to Mauch Chunk...	9

Rate, - - - 75 Cts.

EXCURSION I.
Elmira to Geneva (on Seneca Lake) and return.

		MILES.
Northern Central R. R.	...to Watkins'...	22
Seneca Lake Steamer	...to Geneva...	40
Seneca Lake Steamer	...to Watkins'	40
Northern Central R. R.	...to Elmira...	22

Rate, - - $3.15

EXCURSION Q.
Utica to Trenton Falls and return.

		MILES.
Utica and Black River R. R.	...to Trenton Falls...	17
Utica and Black River R. R.	...to Utica...	17

Rate, - $1.25

EXCURSION B.
Albany to Lake Champlain, *via* Lake George and return.

		MILES.
Saratoga Division, Del. & Hud. C. Co's Line	...to Saratoga...	38
Saratoga Division, Del. & Hud. C. Co's Line	...to Glen's Falls...	23
Stage	...to Lake George.	9
Lake George Steamer	...to Baldwin...	36
Saratoga Division, Del. & Hud. C. Co's Line	...to Ft. Ticonderoga...	5
Saratoga Division, Del. & Hud. C. Co's Line	...to Saratoga...	61
Saratoga Division, Del. & Hud. C. Co's Line	...to Albany...	38

Rate, - - - $9.35

EXCURSION C.
Albany to Lake Champlain and return, *via* Lake George.

		MILES.
Saratoga Division, Del. & Hud. C. Co's Line	...to Saratoga...	38
Saratoga Division, Del. & Hud. C. Co's Line	...to Ft. Ticonderoga...	61
Saratoga Division, Del. & Hud. C. Co's Line	...to Baldwin...	5
Lake George Steamer	...to Caldwell...	36
Stage	...to Glen's Fall	9
Saratoga Division, Del. & Hud. C. Co's Line	...to Saratoga...	23
Saratoga Division, Del. & Hud. C. Co's Line	...to Albany...	38

Rate, - - - $9.35

EXCURSION X. 36
Port Kent to Au Sable Chasm and return.

		MILES.
Stage	...to Au Sable Chasm...	3
Stage	...to Port Kent...	3

Rate, - - - - 75 Cts.

EXCURSION X. 43.
Montreal to Quebec and return.

		MILES.
Grand Trunk Railway or Royal Mail Line Steamers	...to Quebec...	172
Grand Trunk Railway or Royal Mail Line Steamers	...to Montreal..	172

Rate, - - - - $1.00

SUMMER PLEASURES.

Who would Summer pleasures try,
Let him to the meadows hie;
Let him smell the new-mown hay,
Let him watch the streamlets gay
See the meads in early morn,
See the farmer tend his corn
Hear the milch-cow's evening low,
See the sunset's golden glow.

THE PREACHER'S JOKE.

WHEN preachers do indulge in jokes they generally let off good ones. Here is the last. Away down east a clergyman was recently charged with having violently dragged his wife from a revival meeting and compelled her to go home with him. The clergyman let the story travel on until he had a fair opportunity to give it a broadside. Upon being charged with the offence, he replied as follows: "In the first place, I never attempted to influence my wife in her views, nor her choice of a meeting. Secondly, my wife has not attended any of the revival meetings in Lowell. In the third place, I have not myself attended any of the meetings for any purpose whatever. To conclude, neither my wife nor myself has any inclination to go to those meetings. Finally, I never had a wife."

DERE'S A HEAP O' DIFFERENCE.

"Sambo, what's your opinion of traveling by railway and steamboat?"

"Now you're talkin', boss! Good gracious! I tole you dere's a heap o' difference. When youse on de railroad and an axident happens, you're right dar; but when youse on de steamboat and she busts and blows up, whar are you? dat's de question. I tell you, boss, you're no whar!"

"Look here, Pete," said a knowing darkey to his companion: "don't stan' on de railroad."

"Why, Joe?"

"Kase ef de cars see dat mouf ob yourn, dey will tink it am de depo' an' run rite in!"

PAYING OFF THE LAWYER.

"Well, what do you know about a horse—you a horse doctor?" said an attorney, who had attained a great notoriety for bullying witnesses, in his peculiarly contemptuous and overbearing manner. "No, I don't pretend to be a horse doctor," replied the witness; "but I know a good deal of the nature of the beast." "That means to say you know a horse from a jackass when you see them?" continued the lawyer, in the same style, looking knowingly, and glancing triumphantly at the spectators, with a telegraphic expression, which said, "Now, I've got him on the hip." "Oh, ye-as—just so," drawled out the intended victim, gazing intently at his legal tormentor, "I know the difference, and I'd never take you for a horse!"

A Long Cane.—An American in London was boasting of the immensity of that country, and mentioned, among other wonders, that he himself had seen a *cane a mile long!* "Pray, what kind of a cane was it?" asked the company incredulously. "A *hurrycane*," replied Jonathan, at the same time ejecting a very decided streak upon the stove.

During a dense fog a Mississippi steamboat took landing. A traveller, anxious to go ahead, came to the unperturbed manager of the wheel, and asked why they stopped. "Too much fog. Can't see the river." "But you can see the stars overhead." "Yes," replied the urbane pilot; "but until the biler busts we ain't going that way." The passenger went to bed.

A preacher in one of the fashionable London churches is reported to have said, "St. Paul remarks, and I *partially* agree with him." This reminds us of the judge who, in sentencing a prisoner to death, observed, "Prisoner at the bar, you will soon have to appear before another and *perhaps* a better Judge."

When the cholera was raging in the south of Europe, a native in Hungary heard that in a certain village it attacked men only. Hoping to escape the disease, he disguised himself as a female, and went to live in the favored village. Soon after his arrival, he was attacked with the disorder, and in his agony, exclaimed, "Alas, alas, who could have betrayed my sex!"

"Why does lightning so rarely strike twice in the same place?" Professor Wortman asked the new boy in the class of natural philosophy. "Huh," said the boy "it never needs to." And it is a little singular that nobody had thought of that reason before.

Quebec, etc.—Lake Superior Tours.

EXCURSION X. 67.
Quebec to Ha Ha Bay and return.

		MILES.
Grand Trunk Railway and Steamer	...to Ha Ha B.	56
Grand Trunk Railway and Steamer	...to Quebec	208

Rate, - - - - $8.00

EXCURSION 2560.
Toronto to Lake Couchiching and return.

		MILES.
Northern Railway of Canada	...to Lake Couchiching	87
Northern Railway of Canada	...to Toronto	87

Rate, - - - - $ .6

LAKE SUPERIOR TOURS.

*EXCURSION U. 1.
Buffalo to Sault Ste. Marie and return.

		MILES.
Lake Superior Transit Company's Steamers	to Sault Ste. Marie	600
Lake Superior Transit Company's Steamers	to Buffalo	600

Rate, - - - - $25.00

*EXCURSION U. 2.
Buffalo to Marquette and return.

		MILES.
Lake Superior Transit Company's Steamers	to Marquette	775
Lake Superior Transit Company's Steamers	to Buffalo	775

Rate, - - - - $32.00

*EXCURSION U. 3.
Buffalo to Duluth and return.

		MILES.
Lake Superior Transit Company's Steamers	to Duluth	1150
Lake Superior Transit Company's Steamers	to Buffalo	1150

Rate, - - - - $50.00

*EXCURSION U. 4.
Buffalo to Sault St. Marie and return to Niagara Falls.
(*Via North and South Shores of Lake Superior.*)

		MILES.
Lake Superior Transit Company's Steamers	to Sault St. Marie	600
Collingwood Lake Superior Line Steamers	to Collingwood	400
Northern Railway of Canada	to Toronto	94
Niagara Navigation Co's Steamers	to Lewiston	36
New York Central and Hudson River Railroad	to Niagara Falls	7

Rate, - - - - $26.50

*EXCURSION U. 5.
Buffalo to Duluth and return to Niagara Falls.
(*Via North and South Shores of Lake Superior.*)

		MILES.
Lake Superior Transit Company's Steamers	to Duluth	1150
Collingwood Lake Superior Line Steamers	to Collingwood	950
Northern Railway of Canada	to Toronto	94
Niagara Navigation Co's Steamers	to Lewiston	36
New York Central and Hudson River Railroad	to Niagara Falls	7

Rate, - - - - $50.50

*NOTE.—The sailing of these steamers are so arranged that those portions of the Lake which are passed *at night* on the upward trips, are passed *by daylight* on the return trips, thereby affording a diversity of the most picturesque scenery throughout the entire trip. Holders of these tickets are privileged to stop off at any Lake Superior Port, and to resume their journey by another of the Company's steamers, at pleasure.

STARRUCCA VALLEY.

HERE the picturesque portals of the Susquehanna Valley are opening before him at a spot where Nature has scattered her treasures with a prodigal hand. This is Starrucca, Susquehanna Valley, Pennsylvania. Before the train reaches the foot of the mountain, the great sweep of the road permits a general glimpse of Starruc. The viaduct, one of the grandest engineering feats in this country, its eighteen great arches supported by tall and graceful pillars; the Starrucca creek, fresh and buoyant from struggles in wild mount in gorges, and from leaps and tumbles over many a dizzy ledge.

the glorious curve of the Susquehanna as it flows in from the northward by fringing hills and fertile plains all fall beneath the delighted eye. All, all is beauty and forms the subject of one of the most famous of American paintings, "An American Autumn," by Cropsey. It were a task indeed to tell the grandeur of this scene in words.

SUMMER EXCURSION ROUTES—ADVERTISEMENTS

BATES HOUSE,
RUTLAND, VT.
J. M. HAVEN, Proprietor.

BOARD, $2.00 PER DAY.

COMMERCIAL TRAVELLERS in particular, will find this House a desirable place to stop at, as its location is in the very center of the business of Rutland, and has every facility for the commercial man, including roomy and accessible Sample Rooms. First-class Livery connected with the House.

"On the Raymondskill."

THE RAMAPO VALLEY.

There are few more romantic localities than that part of the Valley of the Ramapo which is traversed by the Erie Railway. Eleven lakes, perched high on the mountains that are a distinguishing characteristic of this portion of New York state, send their tumbling outlets into the valley and form the stream known as the Ramapo River. There are forty of these lakes within a few miles of the spot where the Erie Railway enters the valley. The en'rance is made at Suffern, through a great gap in the Hudson Highlands, which extend north-east-ward, in rugged peaks, some of them 1,800 feet in height. The railroad presents the ever varying scenery of the valley to the tourist for a distance of 16 miles. The river courses meadows and ravines, tumbles over rocky bottom, and spreads out here and there into beautiful lakes. Fixed ledges of lofty rock, and huge piles of enormous boulders tower above and lie along its borders. No region is more interesting historically. Among its attractions is the bold mountain peak, near Ramapo Station, known as the Torne. Upon the summit of this mountain General Washington stood, while the American troops were quartered in the valley during the Revolution, and surveyed the movements of the British fleet in the New York harbor. There are numerous buildings still standing that were built before the Revolution, and many relics of fortifications and encampments, between Suffern and Sloatsburg. The region is the very home of health. Its air is especially antagonistic to bronchial and lung diseases. It is the same air that makes the Cornwall mountains, on the Hudson, the favorite retreat of invalids. Good hotels and boarding houses may be found at any of the Erie Railway stations in the valley.

MINNEWASKA AND AWASTING.

Among the highest and raggedest peaks of the Shawangunk mountains, in Ulster county, N. Y., where only a few years since the foot of man had seldom trod, are a number of most remarkable and charming lakes. One of these, Lake Mohonk, has been accessible for several years, and tourists and permanent summer guests have found an excellent stopping place at the large hotel there. It was only a year or two ago, however, that a still grander resort was made known to the outside world. This is Lake Minnewaska, perched on the rocky crest of a Shawangunk peak, near "Sam's Point," the great mural height that overlooks the entire Wall-kill Valley, immediately beneath it, and commands an unobstructed view of the greater part of the Eastern and Middle States. Minnewaska has a lovely companion in Lake Awasting, near by, the outlet of which leaps over a precipice 100 feet in height, forming a cataract of beauty and grandeur. Our Artist's pencil describes these rare Ulster county mountain retreats in a more pleasing and satisfactory manner than can be done with the pen. They are reached by a most enjoyable drive, on a way that commands as many wonderful glimpses of scenery as any of the famous White Mountain drives. The railroad station is New Paltz, N. Y., reached by the Erie Railway direct.

A RAILROAD IN THE CLOUDS.

The most novel and pleasurable summer excursion route in this country is that offered by the New York, Lake Erie and Western Railway over the famous "Gravity Roads" of Northern Pennsylvania. These Railroads are a series of inclined planes, and reach an altitude of 2,500 feet above tide.. They traverse a country of rugged mountains and glens; waterfalls, gorges, streams and valleys greet the tourist in magnificent variety. One of these novel roads connects with the Erie at Honesdale, Pa. It is owned by the Delaware and Hudson Canal Company, and climbs the Moosic mountains to Carbondale by one route, and returns to Honesdale by another—both offering continuous delight to the tourist. The sketch of the "Shepherd's Crook" in another place, which is a view of this road, will give an idea of the character of the scenery along the route. This "crook" is the most abrupt curve ever attempted in railroad building in this country. The Honesdale Gravity Road is 16 miles in length in one direction and 20 in the other. It was the first railroad constructed in this country for actual transportation business, having been completed in 1829. The other road of this kind open to Erie tourists extends from Hawley, Pa., to Scranton, and is the property of the Pennsylvania Coal Company. It offers a round trip of 70 miles. It also climbs the lofty Moosic range. The scenery is inde-scribably grand. The peculiarity of these roads is the absence of locomotives in running trains, hence the entire freedom from cinders, dust and smoke. They are equipped with luxuriant coaches of miniature patterns, and with open excursion cars. The trains run up hill and down at the rate of 25 miles an hour. At the points where the summits of the mountains are reached the view from the cars embraces a panorama extending over thousands of square miles of the most beautiful country. Both roads take the tourist into the heart of the romantic Lacka-wanna Coal region.

SUBURBAN HOMES.

For a distance of 30 miles the New York, Lake Erie and Western Railroad extends through a country especially adapted in every way to the wants of those who, while engaged in business in New York and neighboring cities, desire to live amid the quietude and healthful surroundings of suburban retreats. Within the distance named the road traverses the fairest portions of three historic and picturesque valleys—the Passaic, the Paramus and the Ramapo. The advantages offered in these localities for rural homes have already been seized by thousands, but there is still room for thousands more among the fields, hills, streams and lakes of the region. Choice building sites are in the market constantly at very reasonable prices and terms; cottages, ready for occupancy, can readily be secured by tenants, or purchased at low rates; and parties who prefer to board may be accommodated the year around at convenient, pleasant and home-like hotels or private residences. No other road running out of New York offers so many attractions to seekers after suburban homes as the Erie. The stations included in this near-by territory are as follows, with their distances from Jersey City:

Rutherford Park, 9 miles; Passaic, 12 miles; Clifton, 14 miles; Lake View, 15 miles; Paterson, 17 miles; Hawthorne, 19 miles; Ridgewood, 22 miles; Hohokus, 24 miles; Allendale, 26 miles; Ramsey's, 28 miles; Mahwah, 30 miles; Suffern, 32 miles.

There are the best of schools and churches of all denominations in these places, and vital statistics show the entire region to be one of extraordinary healthfulness.

MOUNTAIN RESORTS.

The New York, Lake Erie and Western Railroad is peculiarly favored by the country through which it passes in the matter of those resorts which are always most in demand during the summer months—resorts among the mountains. The Hudson River Highlands, the Schunemunk, the Comfort Hills, the Shawangunks, and the lofty Catskill, spurs of the Delaware valley, are all made easy and quick of access by this road. *The Highlands*, which are encountered at Suffern, 32 miles from New York, are followed for 19 miles by the Newburgh Short Cut branch of the Erie, which joins the main line at Turners. *Central Valley, Highland Mills, Woodbury, Mountainville, Cornwall, New Windsor* and *Newburgh* are among the resorts visited every year by thousands. They are from 1,500 to 2,000 feet above tide. Forty crystal lakes, on the borders of many of which stand magnificent hotels and cottages, are perched among the ancient crags, on the summits of which these resorts are located. They are stocked with the gamest of fish, and amply supplied with row and sail boats. These Highland retreats are annually sought by sufferers from pulmonary complaints, who find great relief in the pure air of the mountains, many invalids have been completely restored to health by a few seasons spent in among the Highlands. The late N. P. Willis, the poet, was the first to discover the remarkable curative properties of the mountain air of the Highlands, he being himself completely restored to health from an advanced stage of consumption. The historic attractions of the Highlands, especially those of Newburgh and New Windsor, are familiar throughout the country. The full beauty of the Highlands can only be enjoyed by a ride over the Erie branch that follows their rugged sides and penetrates their storied valleys.

THE SCHUNEMUNK MOUNTAINS are a spur of the Highlands, and are the Northern boundary of the Ramapo Valley. *Turner's* Station, with its pleasant surroundings, and *Monroe*, 48 miles from New York, are stations on the Erie from which the many hotels and boarding houses, high on the range of hills are reached.

THE SHAWANGUNK MOUNTAINS cross the state of New York in a north-eastward direction, through the counties of Orange, Sullivan and Ulster. They are a continuation of the Blue Mountains of New Jersey and Pennsylvania. In Northern Ulster they become the famous Catskills. The main line of the New York, Lake Erie and Western Railroad begins the ascent of the Shawangunks 65 miles from New York, and crosses them at Otisville, at an elevation of 1,500 feet above tide. The Montgomery branch of the Erie, from Goshen, reaches the base of the Shawangunks in Ulster county, at New Paltz, 88 miles from New York. In this latter vicinity are some of the highest peaks of the range, Paltz Point, Sky-top, Eagle's Cliff, and others, nearly 3,000 feet high. The resorts among these lofty hills are reached from New Paltz Station. Principal among them are Lake Mohonk and Lake Minnewaska. (*See Lake-side Resorts.*) Easy conveyances run to the summit of the mountains. The road up the mountain commands such sublime views that the steepness of the way is rather a zest than an annoyance. The crags are rugged and the homes of perpetual breeze. From their lofty tops an expanse of country embracing the Wallkill, Rondout and Shawangunk Valleys, the farthest Catskills, the broad Hudson, the great mountain-ranges of the Eastern States, and the distant Alleghanies, is brought beneath the eye. Near Lake Minnewaski is Sam's Point, 2,700 feet in height, and the abrupt terminus of a spur of the range. Its face is a perpendicular bluff of white rock, visible from the main line of the Erie at Otisville, 30 miles distant.

In the Shawangunks, reached by the main line, is Guymard, in a most picturesque spot, and with the attractions of lake and stream, as well as mountain. Guymard Mineral Spring is a great attraction for invalids at this station. There are grand mountain drives about Guymard and a large modern hotel to accommodate guests. The place is 80 miles from New York.

From Port Jervis—itself surrounded by high, breezy summits, several noted summering places among the mountains are reached. By a drive down the Delaware Valley. a drive, by the way, over a natural boulevard, as smooth as a floor, and thirty miles in length. Milford, "the gem of the Delaware," Coneshaugh Springs, Dingman's and Bushkill are reached. These are truly mountain retreats, for turn which way the visitor may, lofty, rugged, wooded hills rise before him, and the breezes that carry health and comfort to him on their wings, he feels could be born only amid the "eternal hills." These places are all noted for the excellence of their hotel and boarding-house accommodations. The drives are unsurpassed anywhere. Within a radius of twenty miles there are no less than *five hundred water-falls*, some of them exceeding any in the Catskills or White Mountains in height and grandeur. Among these may be mentioned those of the Saukill and the Raymondskill Creeks, near Milford; the Dingman Brook and Adams Brook Cataracts, near Dingman's, and the wonderful Falls of the Big and Little Bushkill, near Bushkill. These cataracts are from 50 to 120 feet in height, and the centres of the wildest, weirdest surroundings. These resorts of the lower Delaware have been aptly termed "The Homes of the Cataract." Port Jervis is 88 miles from New York. Milford is 7 miles from Port Jervis; Coneshaugh Spring, 11; Dingman's, 15; Bushkill, 28.

The Port Jervis and Monticello Railroad connects the Erie with the favorite resorts of the Sullivan county mountains. Monticello, 24 miles from Port Jervis, is 1,600 feet above tide. It is one of the most charming villages in the State, and at least 500 city people seek its attractions every year. Sheriff Morris' Mansion House is one of these. Pleasant Lake, a grand sheet of water, is near the village. Nine miles from Monticello, at the same height above tide, is the well-known resort, White Lake, with Mount Wilder, Mount Sherwood, and a host of less prominent peaks surrounding it, and the blue line of the Catskill range filling the distance. Both Monticello and White Lake atmosphere, is a relentless foe to asthma and kindred diseases. (*See Lake-side Resorts.*)

Shohola, with its wonderful streams and glen; *Lackawaxen*, girdled about by hills, and mirrored in the broad Delaware; *Narrowsburg*, with its picturesque old bridge and unfathomable eddy in the river; *Cochecton, Callicoon, Hancock* and *Deposit;* all crowded by the high mountains of the Upper Delaware Valley, offer rare attractions to the lover of the wild and rugged in nature, and of true life among the mountains. Shohola is 107 miles from New York; Lackawaxen, 110 miles; Narrowsburg, 122; Cochecton, 131 miles; Callicoon, 136 miles; Hancock, 164; Deposit, 178. The Glen on the Shohola Creek, at Shohola, is a remarkable collection of natural curiosities, discovered in 1876. Cochecton and vicinity offer a grand field for the antiquarian, as near it was made one of the first white settlements in Pennsylvania, and it became the scene of many of the most bloody and dramatic episodes of the early days. At *Lackawaxen* the Honesdale Branch of the Erie connects with the main line. Honesdale, the western terminus of the Branch, is one of the most interesting and attractive points on the entire road. It is the starting point of one of the celebrated "Railroads in the Clouds," over which tourists are whirled without any visible motive power, over mountains 2,500 feet high. From Hawley, on the Honesdale Branch, another of these wonderful railroads starts. Both roads penetrate the upper coal regions, and offer the most novel and enjoyable tour in this country. (*See "Railroading in the Clouds."*) Wallenpaupack Falls, at Hawley, are a famous attraction to visitors. From *Shohola*, by stage, several resorts in the western Sullivan County mountains are reached, Highland Lake being the most popular. It is seven miles from the Erie Railroad station.

RESORTS FOR THE SPORTSMAN.

No railroad in this country extends through a country so pre-eminently adapted to the wants of the sportsman as the New York, Lake Erie and Western. Almost every station is the centre of

Scene on the Erie Railway.

some attraction for the hunter or the angler. The lover of trouting, bass fishing and pickerel fishing, will find ample fields for the gratification of his passion among the creeks, lakes and rivers during the spring and summer; while the later season opens unrivalled haunts for the hunter, with his fowling-piece or rifle, his setter or deer-hound.

TROUT STREAMS.

The many streams of Sullivan and Delaware Counties, N. Y., and those of Pike County, Pa., are the most convenient, and give the best returns to the angler from the cities. The streams of Susquehanna County, Pa., Bradford County, Pa., Potter County, Pa., Livingston County, N. Y., Steuben County, N. Y., and other border counties, are reached, also, from many stations along the line of the road. The Sullivan County streams are accessible from Middletown, Port Jervis, Shohola, Cochecton, Callicoon, Hancock and intermediate stations. *From Middletown*, the New York Midland Railroad enters Sullivan County. The principal streams are the Neversink and its branches, and these about Fallsburgh, Liberty and Monsston, on that road. *From Port Jervis*, the Bushkill, the Shinglekill and Mongaup Creeks are reached by Monticello Railroad or wagon. *Across the Delaware from Shohola* are Half-way Brook and Beaver Brook, favorite trout waters. *From Cochecton*, Lake Huntington, one of the few lakes in the state that still abound in trout, is reached. It is four miles from the station. *Near Callicoon* are the numerous branches of the Callicoon Creek, noted haunts of the trout. The head-waters of the Beaverkill are easy of access from Callicoon. Basket Brook, Hawkins Creek, near the stations of the same name, are still favorite resorts of the angler. *About Hancock* there are many trout streams, among them Cadosia, Sands, Shehawken, Trout, Tyler and Reed's Creeks. The Beaverkill, Willowemoc and other famous Creeks in the Sullivan and Delaware County wilderness can also be reached easily from Hancock. At all of these places guides, flies, bait, and all kinds of tackle may be readily obtained.

The Creeks of Pike County are near Port Jervis, Shohola, Lackawaxen and Millville stations. From Port Jervis, the Milford, Dingman's and Bushkill Brooks are reached. Within four miles of Milford are the Vandermark, the Sawkill, the Raymondskill, the Capow, and the Coneshaugh, with their branches. The Sawkill and Vandermark flow through the village. It is estimated that 50,000 trout are taken from the Sawkill every year. The streams about Milford are all protected, and anglers are expected to obtain permission of the property owners along them before going upon the creeks. *At Dingman's* are the Adams, the Dingman and the Decker Creeks. The Adams is noted for the large size of its trout and its superb scenery. These streams are from one to five miles distant from the village. *Near Bushkill* are the Saw, Tom's, and the Little and Big Bushkill Creeks. The visiting angler will find at Milford, Dingman's and Bushkill expert local fishermen to conduct him to and along any of the streams. *At Shohola* are the Shohola and Panther Brooks, and near by Taylor's Creek. *Near Lackawaxen* are Lord's Brook, the Shohola, and Taylor's Brook. The streams of Blooming Grove, and the brooks of the Pike county interior wilderness, are accessible. *At Millville*, on the Honesdale Branch, the Blooming Grove Creek enters the Lackawaxen River. Millville is the Blooming Grove Park station. Conveyances run from the Railroad to the Park, seven miles distant, where there are several trout streams.

Conveyances to all of the streams mentioned above can be obtained at the villages near them.

BLACK BASS, PICKEREL, &c.

In the following lakes and streams along the Erie, the best of black bass and pickerel fishing may be enjoyed. Every accommodation in the way of boats and tackle is to be had at the fishing grounds.

Greenwood Lake, on the Greenwood Lake Branch, *all the lakes* in the Highlands of the Hudson, reached by Newburgh Short Cut from Turner's Station (47 miles from New York), and by easy conveyance from that station. The *Walkill River*, at any of the stations along the Montgomery and Pine Island Branches, which join the main line at Goshen (60 miles from New York). *Lake Mohonk and Minnewaska* in the Shawangunk, reached from New Paltz, on the Montgomery Branch. The *Delaware River* at Port Jervis, Milford, Dingman's, Shohola, Lackawaxen, and all the stations along the Delaware Division. *The lakes in the vicinity of Honesdale and Hawley*, on the Honesdale Branch, in Wayne and Pike Counties, Pa. *Blooming Grove Park Lake*, from Millville, on the Honesdale Branch. *Pleasant Lake*, near Monticello; reached from Port Jervis. *White Lake*, Sullivan County, N. Y.; reached from Port Jervis.

Besides black bass and pickerel, *lake trout, muscalonge, salmon, trout and all varieties of bass*, abound in the following lakes:

Seneca and Keuka Lakes; reached from Elmira, and from Bath, via Hammondsport. *Conesus and Hemlock, Honeoye and Canadice Lakes;* reached from Livonia, on the Rochester Division. *Silver Lake;* reached from Gainesville, on the Buffalo Division. *Chautauqua Lake;* reached from Salamanca, on the Western Division.

DEER, PARTRIDGE, WOODCOCK, &c.

The forests of Ulster, Sullivan, Pike and Wayne Counties still offer rare sport to the deer hunter. They may be reached from Middletown, Port Jervis, Monticello, Milford, Shohola, Lackawaxen, Millville, Hawley, Honesdale, Narrowsburg, Callicoon and Hancock. Partridge, woodcock, rabbit, hare and other small game also abounds in those regions. Woodcock, quail, partridge and rabbit shooting is excellent about Goshen, stations on the Pine Island Branch, Warwick and surrounding country. Warwick Woodlands are reached by the Warwick Branch, from Greycourt (54 miles from New York).

LAKE SIDE RESORTS.

Lake Resorts are especially numerous and attractive on the line of the New York, Lake Erie and Western Railway, both near the cities and at a distance. *Greenwood Lake*, the largest sheet of inland water in New York, south of the Central lakes, is only 54 miles from New York city; it is 9 miles long and 2 wide, and is shut in by lofty, wooded, picturesque mountains. The Brandon House, the Windermere House, the Throckmaton House, and others, on the shores of the lake, have become famous resorts. A steamboat plies on the lake.

Summit Lake, near Central Valley (48 miles from N. Y.), *Highland Lake* (50 miles from N. Y.), near Highland Mills, both in the Newburgh Short Cut, are favorite resorts, with fine hotel accommodations. They are in the highlands, 1800 feet above the sea. (*See Mountain Resorts.*)

Lake Mohonk, near New Paltz, on the Montgomery Branch (88 miles from N. Y.) Lake Mohonk is about half a mile long, very deep, and surrounded by precipitous shores and dense forest. There are mountains all about it. Deep caverns abound in the rocks, containing subterranean streams and heaps of ice, whose existence is perpetual in these rocky confines. Best of hotel accommodations.

Lake Minnewaska, near Lake Mohonk. In the most romantic portions of the Shawangunk. Near Lake Awasting, Awasting Falls, and the celebrated ice caves of Ulster County. (*See Mountain Resorts.*)

White Lake; largest body of water in southern New York, except Greenwood; reached from Port Jervis, via Port Jervis and Monticello Branch and stage from Monticello. Seven large hotels and cottages. Favorite resort for invalids. (*See Mountain Resorts.*)

The Central New York Lakes—Seneca Cayuga, Keuka, Canandaigua, and Otsego; the wonders of the Empire state.

The Lakes of Western New York—Chautauqua, Silver, Honeoye, Canadice, Conesus, and Hemlock. These lakes, although of great size, are still mostly surrounded by primitive mountain scenery. Chautauqua—"the gem of western New York"—is now one of the most fashionable and popular resorts in the country. All of these lakes are visited annually by thousands.

www.ingramcontent.com/pod-product-compliance
Lightning Source LLC
Chambersburg PA
CBHW032240080426
42735CB00008B/940